Wings of Hope:
9 Hours, 1 Wing

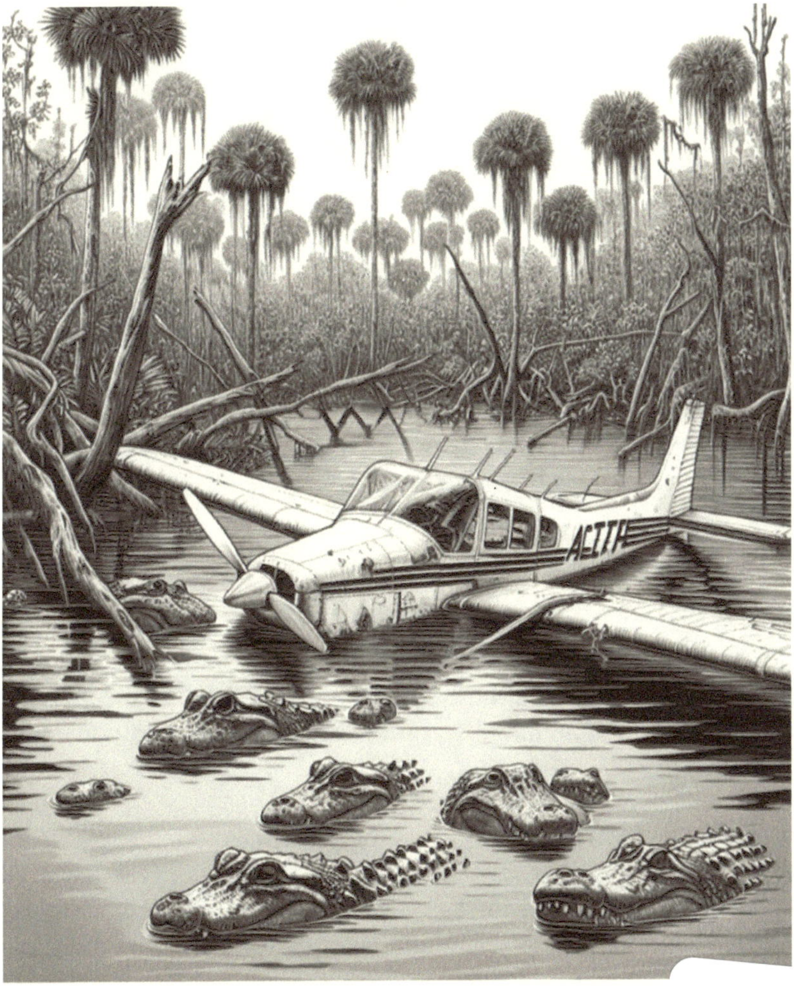

Eshaan Majumdar

INDIA · SINGAPORE · MALAYSIA

Paperback 979-8-89363-348-1
Hardcase 979-8-89363-638-3

This memoir, "Wings of Hope: 9 Hour, 1 Wing. A true story of Pilot's Peril and Resilience in Gator Shadows," is a work of non-fiction based on true events. The characters, incidents, and dialogues are drawn from real-life experiences and have been fictionalized for literary purposes.

It reflects the author's present recollections of experiences. While every effort has been made to ensure accuracy, the author acknowledges that memory is both a faithful companion and a fickle muse. Names, locations, and timelines have been altered to protect privacy and enhance storytelling.

This is a survival story and the author through his experiences is narrating how to be calm under adversity and thrive. The author has deliberately not covered any details of the air crash and the situations leading to the crash as while this book is going into print the investigation to ascertain the reason of the air crash is still under progress.

Wings of Hope:
9 Hours, 1 Wing

Eshaan Majumdar

Edited by

Fia Majumdar

INDIA • SINGAPORE • MALAYSIA

Table of Contents

Acknowledgements

To the unsung heroes who saved me from the jaws of despair—the brave souls of the ***Broward Sheriff Fire Rescue****, who responded swiftly to the distress call. Your courage and determination pulled me from the wreckage, and I owe you, my life.*

To my instructor ***Juan Andres Mugica****, thank you for your exceptional guidance, patience, and expertise throughout my aviation journey. Thank you for being an outstanding mentor and role model inside and outside of the cockpit.*

To my enduring friends and copilots in the U.S., notably ***Mayur, Raghav,*** *and* ***Diya****, who stood by me when the world seemed to crumble. Your unwavering support and friendship were my lifelines in those dark hours.*

I will also dedicate this book to my ***flying school*** *and the* ***owner*** *(name being withheld), it was she who made the first may day call for rescue and it is her support because of which I am alive today.*

To my healers—the ***tireless doctors*** *and* ***nurses*** *in the US and India*[1]*—who stitched my wounds, both physical and emotional. You* *mended broken bones and shattered dreams. Your compassion and expertise breathed life back into me.*

To my friends back in India, notably ***Arjun, Aditya, Pratyush*** *and many more. You guys stood by me and helped me recover mentally and physically. Your support and care were invaluable during those challenging times,*

Cheers boys!

And to my ***Dada****, an Indian Air Force Veteran, whose courage and dedication inspire me daily. To* ***Dadi****,* ***Nana****, and* ***Nani****, whose love envelops me like a comforting embrace. My paternal uncle,* ***Rayhan****, affectionately called 'bare Papa,' not only sponsored part of my training but also stood as a beacon of encouragement. And to my maternal uncle, '****Manu mama****', and my aunt, '****Mikoo massi****', whose blessings, I believe, have always guarded me like celestial angels. Their presence has been my strength, and their love has fueled my resilience.*

And to my dear sister ***Fia****—the silent architect of these words. Your unwavering dedication, keen eye, and unwritten encouragement breathed life into this memoir. This book bears your fingerprints, and its pages whisper your name. But beyond the ink, you stood by me during the quiet hours of recovery—a beacon of unwavering support, a listener to my unspoken fears. For that, I am forever grateful.*

Lastly, to my ***parents****—my pillars of strength. Your love transcends continents, and your unwavering belief in my dreams kept me fighting. This book is dedicated to you—the wind beneath my "****Wings of Hope****."*

May these words echo across time, honouring those who saved, supported, and healed. May their stories intertwine with mine—a testament to survival, resilience, and the indomitable human spirit.

Foreword

In the vast expanse of the *Everglades*, where sawgrass stretches to meet the horizon and the air hangs heavy with secrets, a remarkable tale unfolds—a story of survival, courage, and the indomitable human spirit.

As I read the pages that follow, I am reminded that life's most profound lessons often emerge from the crucible of adversity. The author, who has walked through fire and faced the primal jaws of nature, invites us into his world—a world where the ordinary fractures, revealing the extraordinary.

In these pages, you will encounter more than an account of an air crash or a close encounter with the natural forces of the *Everglades*. You will witness the raw edges of fear, the resilience that defies reason, and the bonds forged in the crucible of chaos. The *Everglades* become a character in their own right—a silent witness to both tragedy and triumph.

What compels us to read such stories? Is it the thrill of danger, the vicarious taste of survival? Perhaps. But deeper still, it is the recognition of our shared vulnerability—the knowledge that life can change in an instant, that fate dances on the edge of a wing, and that hope flickers even in the darkest swamps.

As you turn these pages, remember that memoirs are not mere recollections; they are invitations—to empathy, to understanding, and to reflection. The author's journey becomes our own, and we emerge changed, our hearts echoing the pulse of their courage.

So, dear reader, step into this world of tangled mangroves, where the sun sets like a molten coin and the alligators glide silently. Let the author guide you through the wreckage, where survival is not a choice but a primal instinct. As you emerge on the other side, blinking into the light, know that you, too, have survived—an air crash of emotions, a plunge into the depths of the human experience.

May this memoir be your life raft, your compass, and your sanctuary. For after every dark night, there is a brighter day waiting—a day when we rise from the muck, our spirits unbroken and find solace in the whisper of the soul.

Major DP Singh[2],
India's first Blade Runner and a fellow Aviator

Preface

In the quiet hours before dawn, when the world slumbers and the stars still hold their breath, I sit down to write. These words—the ink-stained echoes of survival—etched upon the fabric of memory, woven from threads of courage and vulnerability.

This memoir is not a chronicle of mere events; it is an excavation of the human spirit. It invites you into the cockpit of turmoil, where altitude and attitude collide. Here, the *Everglades* become more than a swamp; they become a canvas for resilience, a stage for primal instincts.

As you turn these pages, you will walk alongside me—the survivor, the witness, the seeker. You will taste the salt of fear, the grit of determination, and the sweetness of hope. You will meet the alligators, not as reptilian adversaries, but as ancient guardians of forgotten wisdom.

Why share this story? Because we are all survivors—of crashes, of heartaches, of our own flawed humanity. We cling to life's wreckage, gasping for air, and in those desperate moments, we discover what truly matters. We find solace in the whisper of the soul, the quiet knowing that there is light beyond the darkness.

So, dear reader, fasten your seatbelt. We are about to take flight—through dreams, love, and starlit skies, across the threshold of fear. And when we emerge on the other side, battered but unbroken, may you find your own reflections in these pages. For after every dark night, there is a brighter day waiting—a day when we rise, not as victims, but as witnesses to our own resilience.

Welcome to the Everglades. Welcome to survival.

Welcome to Wings of Hope

"अविनाशि तु तद्विद्धि येन सर्वमिदं ततम्।[3]"

"Understand that which is indestructible by which all this is pervaded."

Prologue

तं विद्याद् दुःखसंयोगवियोगं योगसंज्ञितम्।
स निश्चयेन योक्तव्यो योगोऽनिर्विण्णचेतसा।।[4]

(Detachment from pain and pleasure leads to true yoga. By practicing with unwavering determination and a steady mind, one can rise above suffering)

I plummet toward the murky expanse of the *Everglades*, wrestling with the controls. Beads of cold sweat slide down my back as I mutter frantic prayers. The altimeter unwinds at a sickening pace, no matter how hard I pull at the yoke; my terrifying descent continues unchecked.

Just before impact, a lightning bolt sears downward, branching through the storm clouds to illuminate the marshlands for one fleeting second. In that flash, I glimpse the full horror of my situation—miles of trackless swampland brimming with predators—lurking in the murky waters.

The plane plunges into the water with a deafening splash. The cockpit shudders, metal screeching as the wings almost tear away. Black water floods through the jagged holes, rising swiftly to my chest and neck.

In the murky abyss of that fateful night, my senses blurred, and the world narrowed to a desperate struggle. The buckles, once my lifeline, now conspired against me. Eventually they yielded, but my right foot remained ensnared in a cruel trap of pain and panic.

The choice was stark: surrender to the murky depths alongside the wreckage or defy fate. My mind raced, fuelled by adrenaline and desperation. I felt the twisted metal, the remnants of what was once a soaring machine. It held no salvation, only the promise of a watery grave.

And so, with a primal scream, I chose defiance. My trembling hands tore at my own flesh, sinew yielding to resolve. The agony was eclipsed by the primal urge to survive. I saw the raw muscles of my calf, a heel dangling like a macabre ornament. Blood mingled with swamp water as I wrenched myself free.

Gasping for air, I tried to pull myself to onto the wing of the plane but with one dangling heel and countless bruises all over my body it seemed like I didn't have the strength to pull myself fully over the wing. The inky night swallowed me whole, and I strained my eyes, seeking any sign of rescue. But there was no celestial light, no guiding star. Only the endless expanse of swampland, indifferent to my struggle and the gators, those ancient predators, they were not indifferent. They circled, their eyes glinting like shards of obsidian. Their hunger was palpable, primal—a dance of death in the moonlit waters. I could feel their presence, their anticipation. They sensed my vulnerability, my struggle—their next meal.

One slid closer, its scaled hide brushing against the plane's torn metal. Its eyes locked onto mine, unblinking. I could see the hunger—the primal need to consume. Its jaws opened, revealing rows of serrated teeth, and I knew this was the moment of reckoning.

With a surge of resolve, I pulled with all my strength from the sinking fuselage to the wing of the plane. Pain flared in my injured leg, but I kept pushing and pulling—each push a battle against the current and my own mortality. The gators followed, their sinuous bodies cutting through the water. They were relentless, hungry, and patient.

I reached the top of the wing, blood oozing from my wounds. The gators lingered, their eyes never leaving me. I had escaped their jaws, but their presence haunted me. I was now part of an ancient dance—a survivor, marked by primal scars.

The *Everglades* whispered their secrets—the haunting cries of unseen creatures, the weight of solitude. Salvation remained elusive, yet I clung to hope. For in that forsaken wilderness, perhaps courage would be enough to carry me through the night, inch by agonizing inch, toward an uncertain dawn.

I woke up from a dream, my body sweaty and my heart racing. The nightmare had let go of me eventually.

At night, my soul felt sad. It remembered old times that didn't want to go away. In bed, covered by moonlight, I was trapped in a dream that felt real. In that dream, I was *Eshaan*, just 19 and a pilot with dreams bigger than the sky.

I sat on the edge of my bed, trembling, as a haunting question echoed in my mind, one that would continue to haunt me in the dead of night:

"Did I lose more than my plane that night? Or did I gain something that would change my life forever?"

This is the story of how I survived the crash, and how I learned to fly again.

That which does not kill us makes us stronger

SEAGULL

CHAPTER 1
THE GENESIS OF A DREAM

"MANN TRACHT, UN GOTT LACHT"[5]
(MAN PLANS and GOD LAUGHS)

"कर्मण्येवाधिकारस्ते मा फलेषु कदाचन |
"मा कर्मफलहेतुर्भूर्मा ते संगोऽस्त्वकर्मणि ||"[6]

(You have a right to perform your prescribed duties, but you are not entitled to the fruits of your actions. Never consider yourself the cause of the results of your activities, and never be attached to not doing your duty)

He walked into the classroom with a confident smile, his eyes sparkling with anticipation. He had aced every exam, every assignment, every project in the senior school. He had been the undisputed topper for six consecutive years. He had no doubt that he would clinch the Gold

Medal today. He took his seat, waiting for the teacher to announce the result. He glanced at his classmates, feeling a mix of pity and pride. They had no chance against him. He was the best.

He planned. God laughed.

The teacher cleared his throat, holding a sheet of paper. "The results are in," he said, scanning the room. "And the winner of the Gold Medal is..." He paused for dramatic effect. "Riya Sharma!"

A collective gasp filled the air, followed by a thunderous applause. He felt his smile freeze, his eyes widen, his heart sink. He looked at Riya, who was beaming with joy, holding the medal in her hand. He looked at the teacher, who was smiling with approval. He looked at his classmates, who were cheering and congratulating Riya. He looked at himself, who was stunned and speechless. He had bagged the second position for the first time in the past six years of his schooling.

He missed it in the final year.

She had always dreamed of studying abroad, of exploring new cultures and opportunities, of making a difference in the world. She had worked hard throughout her school years, excelling in academics, sports, and extracurricular activities. She had applied to the top universities in the *US*, *UK*, and *Canada*, confident that she would get a full scholarship. She had outsourced the best of SOPs and essays, paying a hefty sum to professional writers. She had assured her parents that she would ace the interview, that she would make them proud. She had packed her bags, booked her tickets, and bid farewell to her friends.

She planned. God laughed.

She checked her email every day, hoping for a positive response. She waited for the phone call, the one that would change her life. She waited for weeks, then months, then years. She never got the call. She never got the scholarship. She never got the chance to study abroad.

She is still awaiting the interview call.

These are just a few examples from a student's life, but they are not uncommon or rare. They happen all the time, to everyone. And still we plan. We plan our career, our relationships, our future. We plan as if we have control over our lives, as if we know what lies ahead. But do we? Is planning a futile exercise then? Should we leave everything to destiny or fate, whatever you may call it? The best of planning can fail beautifully, in the most unexpected manner and at the most undesirable moment in your life.

No.

It means we should plan with humility, dream with courage, and live with gratitude. It means we should accept the uncertainty of life and embrace the surprises that come our way. It means we should learn from our failures and celebrate our achievements. It means we should trust in God's plan and cooperate with His will.

I think it happens because we create an illusory world around us where we are the sole superior beings dwelling. This happens because we perceive events asymmetrically. We credit our successes to our skills, and our failures to bad luck.

That is what I learned from my own experience, from my own journey, from my own dream.

A dream that began when I was a child, fascinated by the wonders of the sky. A dream that grew when I was a teenager, inspired by the stories of the pilots. A dream that became a reality when I was a young adult, flying my first solo.

A dream that almost ended when I was 19, crashing into the *Everglades*.

This is the story of how I planned to fly, and how God laughed.

This is the story of how I crashed and survived, and how I learned to soar.

** The Illusion of Control **

I read an interesting fact while I was in the hospital recovering. Researchers found out that 90% of drivers think they are better than the average driver and most students think they are more intelligent than the average student. I was amused by this statistic. How could so many people be so deluded and overconfident? How could they ignore reality and the evidence? How could they believe that they were special and superior?

But then I realized that I was no different. I had also fallen for the illusion of control, the belief that I could plan and predict my life, that I could achieve and succeed without any obstacles or setbacks, that I could be the master of my own destiny. I had also thought that I was a little special, that I had a unique talent and a grand purpose, that I had a bright and glorious future.

But I was wrong. Life proved me wrong. God proved me wrong.

He laughed at my plans. He laughed at my dreams. He laughed at my life.

** The Test of Fate **

I now believe that life takes you in the direction you are destined for, but fate may disrupt the speed of your journey. The universe or God, whatever you may call it, will test you, pose challenges and hinder your progress at some point in your life. You will face difficulties and dangers, failures and frustrations, losses, and regrets. You will feel pain and sorrow, fear and anger, doubt, and despair. You will wonder why this is happening to you, what you did wrong, what you could have done differently.

But you cannot afford to lose sight of the goal you had set for yourself, nor can you waste time cribbing or crying over spilled milk.

The only option left with you is to forge ahead in life, making the best effort that you can to come out of the adverse situation. If you are honest in your efforts and time is favourable, you shall succeed.

That is what I did. That is what I learned. That is what I want to share.

** This is the story of my life, as I lived it **

I was a private pilot when I faced the most terrifying ordeal of my life. It was the night of October 31, 2023, Halloween night. But there was nothing fun or festive about it. It was a night of horror, despair, and struggle. A dark night that seemed to be the longest one I have experienced so far. The pitch darkness around me created hurdles which I did overcome eventually. Something went horribly wrong. Something that I still can't explain. Something that nearly killed me. I crashed in the *Everglades*, I was trapped and injured, alone but surprisingly not afraid. I had no idea if anyone was looking for me, or if anyone would find me. I thought I was going to die. But I didn't. I lived. For nine long hours, I fought for my life, I lived. And I learned. I learned how precious and fragile life is, and how much I wanted to share my story with the world.

To understand who I am, I need to introduce my family members and describe the place they hold in my life.

My father, a military veteran retired early from the Army and now works for the largest Ecom company of the Universe. Some of the survival instinct which I could display in *Everglades*, I feel comes from him.

In the quiet corners of our home, where sunlight dances through lace curtains, my mother's presence weaves a tapestry of resilience. Her left leg, touched by the memory of childhood poliomyelitis, carries a story known only to her—a secret whispered between bone and muscle.

Yet, she wears her uniqueness with grace, as if it were a rare gem hidden beneath layers of fabric. In all my growing up years, her confidence and aura makes up for everything and I have till date, not noticed the subtle cadence of her steps. She moves through life with a quiet strength, a force that refuses to be defined by conventional measures. When others falter, she stands tall, a beacon of courage. Her love knows no bounds; it spills over, embracing us all.

I owe her more than words can convey. She is not merely my mother; she is my compass, pointing toward resilience, compassion, and unwavering love. Her legacy is etched in the way I face adversity—with a quiet determination, a refusal to be defeated. She taught me that strength lies not in conformity, but in the audacity to bloom despite the odds.

My sister, *Fia*, is two years older to me and my best friend. She taught me fun, creativity, and support. She showed me how to be playful and adventurous, how to be imaginative and expressive, how to be loyal and helpful. She also gave me the companionship and the comfort that I needed, especially when I was recovering from the crash. She is always there for me, to make me laugh and to cheer me up, to listen to me and to understand me, to hug me and to heal me.

But my birth was not smooth and easy, in fact, it almost didn't happen. Yes, you heard that right. I am a child who my parents had decided to abort. But something happened on the abortion table that changed their minds.

My parents had a happy love marriage, which started in a dramatic way, but that's another story for later. They had their first child, *Fia*, in 2002. Post that my mom conceived me approximately one a half years after her birth, my parents became sceptical about raising two young children. They mutually decided to terminate the pregnancy.

On the planned date of my abortion, my mother was lying on the operation table, the doctor had already administered her with anaesthesia. As she was drifting into unconsciousness, she had a sudden flash of intuition. A feeling that something was wrong. A vision that something was alive. She saw me. The baby in her womb. She saw me clearly, even though her eyes were blurred. She felt me. The connection that only a mother can feel. She knew me. The child that she was about to kill.

She panicked. She screamed. She begged the doctor to stop. But he ignored her. He thought she was delirious. He told her to calm down and cooperate. He said it was too late to change her mind.

But she wouldn't listen. She wouldn't let him touch her. She called for my father, who was waiting outside. He heard her cries and ran inside. He saw her in distress and asked her what was wrong. She told him what she saw. She told him what she felt. She told him what she knew. She told him to save me.

He looked at her with disbelief. He looked at the doctor with doubt. He thought about me with wonder. He didn't know what to do. He didn't know what to think. He didn't know what to say.

But he knew one thing. He loved her. And he trusted her. And he respected her.

So, he did what she asked for. He told the doctor to stop. He told the doctor to cancel the abortion. He told the doctor to save me.

And he did.

And that's how I was born.

My paternal uncle is an anaesthetist. He wasn't part of the medical team that delivered me, but he had easy access to the OT. He was the one who brought me out of the delivery room and handed me over to my father. He was also the one who gave me my name, Eshaan, which means the lord of the North-East direction. He said it was a fitting name for me, since I was born in the North-East of India, and since I had a miraculous birth.

My mother recalls that I seldom cried as a baby, but I learned to speak quite late, around two years of age. I was a quiet and content child, who didn't demand much attention from them. I didn't even cry for feed, which is surprising, considering how much I love food. My mother explained that I was too busy playing with my toys, especially the mechanical ones. I have been fascinated by them since I was a toddler. I loved to take them apart and put them back together. I loved to pretend that I was fixing things around the house. I had a toolbox full of imaginary tools, and a catchphrase that I repeated: "*theek karna padega*" (It needs to be mended)."

The story of my life is also full of signs. Signs that pointed me to my destiny. Signs that I didn't understand until later. Signs that I followed without knowing. Signs that led me to the sky. Ever since I was a child, I had a passion for flying. A passion that was born with me and grew with me. A passion that made me who I am today. A budding pilot.

My parents tell me that the first word uttered by me was '*Haiyaacopter*' (me trying to say 'helicopter'). That's how much I loved flying. I was fascinated by anything that could fly. My favourite toys were building blocks, Legos, and action figures. But the most memorable was the toy helicopter, one of my prized possessions in class one or two. I would play with it for hours, making it soar and spin in the air. I would pretend that I was the pilot and that I was going on adventures around the world. I would dream of flying a real helicopter someday and feeling the wind in my hair and the freedom in my soul.

I was born in *Silchar*, Assam[7] but I don't remember much of the years spent there, but I know that my birth there was not a coincidence. *Silchar* is a place of history and culture. It is the site of the world's first polo club and the first competitive polo match. It is also the place where, in 1995, an Air India flight from *Kolkata* to *Silchar* became the world's first all-women crew flight. I think that was amazing and inspiring. I think that was a sign. I had also developed a fondness for riding at a young age. I love horses, and at one point, I wanted to be a polo player. I even won a medal in the Junior Novice in riding at the 'Agram Riding Club' [8]. I remember begging my parents to buy me a horse and to send me to *Gurugram*[9] for coaching. But they refused. They said it was too expensive and too dangerous. They had different plans for me seeing my interest in flying. They said I had to focus on my studies and my future. They said I had to be realistic. They understood where my real passion and calibre lay. But this unexpected detour to become a polo player was also no sudden craze, as I have been an animal lover right from my childhood.

Another integral feature that marks my character is my love for animals. They do not scare me. In fact, they make me happy. My love for animals started in *Zakhama*[10](a place in Nagaland close to *Kohima*), where we moved after *Silchar*, when my father was posted there. I petted my first guinea pig there. Now our house is like a mini zoo. From elegant Persian cats to turtles which have now grown massively over the years and are currently at least twenty times bigger. Casper, a Bichon Frisé11, a friendly lapdog, who loves to play and cuddle with me. The most intelligent and ferocious of all being Leo, a golden blue Macaw whose screams are the last thing you want to hear early in the morning.

Apart from my love for animals. I also had a natural inclination towards machines. I loved to tinker with them, and to make them work. I received my first battery-operated motorcycle when I was two years old. I rode it around the house, pretending that I was a racer. I received my first real bike, 'Forty-Eight' a Harley Davidson Sportster series of bikes, when we moved to *Bangalore*, now *Bengaluru*[11] It was the best gift ever. I loved to ride it. I loved to feel alive.

But I also learned to feel pain. I had my first accident on that bike, and it was not pretty. I was riding to my friend's house, when it skidded severely, and I fell and rolled to the other corner of the road. Thankfully, I had the helmet on, which saved my life. But I broke my front incisor, as my teeth struck against the hard metallic helmet. The pain was unbearable. The treatment was traumatic. The memory is still fresh.

But I didn't give up. I didn't stop riding. I didn't stop dreaming.

The story of my life is full of adventure. Adventure that runs in my blood. Adventure that comes from my parents. Adventure that leads me to the sky. My parents had a daring and unconventional marriage. A marriage that crossed the boundaries of religious faith and culture. A marriage that faced many challenges and obstacles. A marriage that inspired me to follow my dreams.

My father is from *Assam*, and my mother is a Punjabi from *Patiala*[12]. By birth, they differ from each other culturally and follow different beliefs. They met at Punjab University, *Chandigarh*[13], where they were classmates and fell in love. They continued their courtship for six years, despite knowing that their tying the knot would not be an easy affair. My father completed his Honours degree in Biophysics and joined the Indian Army, while my mother continued with her studies. Their marriage was a dramatic and romantic story worthy of a *Bollywood* movie. My father, his brother, and some friends from the army were the only people who had attended their wedding.

My adventurous streak also came from my paternal grandfather, who was in the Indian Air Force. He was a brave and skilled Flight Engineer who was part of many missions and won many medals. He passed on his love for flying to my father, who passed it on to me.

Coming back to my growing years, the most memorable years that shaped my personality were those spent in *Bengaluru*. That's where we moved after travelling to various other places where my father was posted. He was part of the elite group of the army fraternity, he toiled, and we had a comparatively privileged and comfortable life. We also had access to more adventurous sports like horse riding, polo, golf, and tennis. But the sport that I loved the most was flying. Flying had been my passion since childhood and had turned into an obsession by this time. Flying was my life.

Since my father's posting to *Bengaluru*, I have visited various Flying Clubs and flying fields where the hobby RC[14] pilots fly their small planes. It was the place where I learned to fly RC planes and where I felt the most alive. It was the place where I met my friends and where I made many memories. It was the place where I started my journey of flying and where I reached my destiny.

I started flying remote-controlled aircrafts when I was eight years old and was amazed. I loved to watch them and to make them soar and glide. I loved to fly them with my father and to learn everything about them. I loved to feel the wind and the freedom. I flew them so deftly that it baffled everyone, even the experienced aircraft flyers. They said I had a natural talent and a keen eye. They said I had a gift and a future. They said I had a sign. A sign that I was born to be a pilot.

And they were right.

But my dream of becoming a pilot was not without challenges. Later, when I was in grade twelve and finally had to enrol in college, my father researched how one could become a commercial pilot in *India* and abroad. We all zeroed down on *Florida* as there are many prestigious flying schools with a fleet of aircrafts and clear weather throughout the year.

I cleared the written exams, and a medical test was held in March. I was finally travelling to *Florida* in May of 2023 and enrolled in one of the flying schools. I was excited and nervous. I was ready and eager. I was living my dream.

Now when I think of it, *Florida* was the place that set me on the path of self-discovery. It was the place where I learned to fly and where I almost died. It was the place where I fulfilled my dream and faced my nightmare. It was the place where I grew and, changed. It was the place where I became a pilot as well as a survivor.

** My Path to Self-Discovery **

The path to self-discovery cannot be an easy one. *Nelson Mandela* in his book 'A Long Walk to Freedom' states that people who have faced extreme situations of adversity alone can build strong characters. People who have never faced challenges or preferred to take the easy path can never do anything outstanding and those who stand at the verge of a catastrophe must use all the courage it takes to balance the situation.

But did I become stronger? Did it really build my character? How did I face the challenges and the catastrophes? A lot depends on how you have grown up. My upbringing has taught me that the single way to grow and become who you want to be is by taking imperfect action. The beauty of the situation is that, at that moment one does not realise that it is not the right decision. For instance, when I was given my Harley Davidson at such an early age, there were many who criticised my parents for that, and even more harshly when I met with an accident, but my family did not feel guilty for it neither did they regret their decision. Accidents are bound to happen. People with an adventurous streak take risks and do not regret when things go wrong at times. The best of decisions taken under the present circumstances, may later turn out to be the most ridiculous or indiscreet ones, but no one does that deliberately. Therefore, there is no scope for remorse when a decision fails or lands you in trouble. On the contrary, the greater the risk the better it is.

At the same time, thinking that all the decisions taken by you will always be right is being overconfident. So, a person who is ready to accept that the decision once taken did not turn out to be the right one and does not regret it, is one who sets oneself on the path to self-discovery. To be adequately educated about your endeavours is an essential prerequisite for self-discovery. Theory and practical–both aspects are essential. But a known fact is that without action no change can be brought out. We must practice. We must get our hands and feet dirty. We need to apply ideas to our lives to-perfectly or imperfectly. In case of a perfect action, we can rejoice and celebrate but in case of an imperfect one, one must understand that learning must go on.

My experience of taking the night flight turned bitter but that alone has made me discover my true self. I learned how to survive, how to recover, and how to fly again. I learned how to be resilient, how to be optimistic, and how to be grateful. I learned how to be myself.

We must move towards what we want from our lives. Others cannot be guiding us through our lives. Someone else cannot decide what is a good idea for us. It is because we alone understand why it matters to us, how it aligns with our vision of life. One can choose to live stuck in fear and complacency and wait until we see the whole path ahead of us. We can also refer to the goalposts erected by others to feel confident and competent to play safe. Still, I believe, confidence and competence come in action. In imperfect action, to be even more precise.

I also discovered that I am a courageous boy, and I did not become one overnight. I had been gathering courage since childhood. Courage is the ability to face any dangerous or painful situation. Courage can be physical or moral. Physical courage is when one can face any physical pain. Moral courage is to do the right things in every situation.

One of the incidents that showed my courage was when I was tending to a street dog who was injured. I went near the dog to apply some medicine on the wounds when it attacked me. It must have felt threatened by my presence and bit me badly. I screamed in pain but did not feel any anger for the wounded dog. I felt pity for the dog. I ran to the physician on the campus and got myself treated for the dog bite without even letting my parents know about it. Along with that, I requested the veterinary doctor to look after the dog. I enquired later that the dog had been carried to the dispensary where it was treated. It was only the next day that my dad had come to know about it when the doctor happened to meet Dad while strolling in the evening.

Courage comes from many things. Some people have courage in them, and some people learn it. Confidence plays an important role. One can face a difficult situation when one is confident about one's skills.

I was born into a family where I dreamt to be a pilot as my skills were, knowingly or unknowingly, being honed for that. This I can see with clarity now when I chose to write my story. I can see now that I was destined to reach *Florida* to meet my fate.

I had planned to be a pilot at a very young age and knew no obstacle could stop me from doing just that. I did not have the faintest idea that things could change drastically in one night.

I was in cloud nine as everything was proceeding just my way, the way I had planned things with Dad. We were least aware of the fact that things could go wrong. In fact, the thought of something going awry was not in our wildest of dreams, something unheard of. Everything had fallen into its right place. We all were so delighted, as a small happy family, content and lucky.

Once I was reading a magazine at the flying club in Bengaluru about driving and I came across these words by *George Carlin* "Have you ever noticed that anybody driving slower than you is an idiot, and anyone going faster than you is a maniac?" In this witty remark, Carlin highlights our tendency to judge others based on our own perspective. When someone drives slower than us, we perceive them as clueless or incompetent. Conversely, when someone speeds past us, they become reckless and dangerous in our eyes.

Perhaps it's a reminder that our judgments are often subjective and influenced by our own experiences. I was in the same state of mind while I was preparing to clear the exams for flying both in *India* and *Florida*. According to me, I was the best, doing just the right thing, at the right pace and no one could have been 'more right' than me.

We were planning. God was laughing.

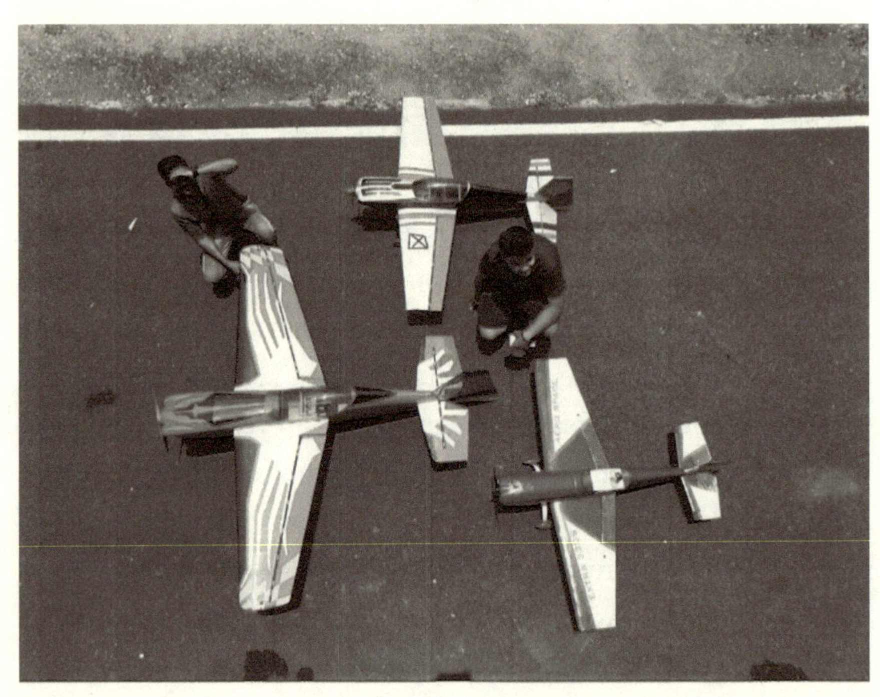

CONGRATS
Eshaan!. AYAAN
Congrats
DALLE
Homestead traffic.
Skyhawk 810F zzzzzz.....
CONGRATS
-ESHAAN DALLE!!!
-RAKS
CONGRATS
ESHAAN!!!
-ALPNA
CONGRATS
-URVAN
First
Solo!!!
12-7-23
FLY HIGH
eshaan
DALLEEE
CONGRATS
SEYY GREAT
JOB! -Jeh.
Congrats!!
Daddy is proud
of you!!
Amazing Job!!
Very proud
of you!!
CONGRATS!
HIGH SKIES
-PATEL KS
N810FS
congrats dale!
You did good :)
-Diya
BORN
AV8R
SKY IS NOT
THE LIMIT
KEEP
SOARING
HIGH
LOVE
ARUN
N810FS
CONGRATS!!!
-CHRISTIAN

CHAPTER 2
THE CAREFREE DAYS

बुद्धिर्ज्ञानमसम्मोह: क्षमा सत्यं दम: शम: |
सुखं दु:खं भवोऽभावो भयं चाभयमेव च ||[15]

(Courage lies in unwavering devotion and knowledge.
When the mind is absorbed in the divine, fear dissipates,
and one becomes aligned with their true self)

Have you ever wondered what it takes to be a pilot? How much courage, skill, and responsibility are involved in flying a plane? I learned these lessons the hard way, on a night flight that changed my life forever.

Ever since I was a kid, I dreamed of being a pilot. I loved watching planes soar in the sky, and I imagined myself in the cockpit, feeling the thrill of flying. I decided in ninth grade that I would be a pilot when I grew up. The only question was whether I wanted to join the

Indian Air Force like my grandpa or not. I admired his bravery and dedication but at that point of time I didn't have the courage to go through the gruel. Also, I wanted to embrace my dream as soon as possible and commercial flying seemed to meet all those expectations and to learn flying in *Florida* was even more attractive. So, I followed my inner calling and enrolled in my dream school in *Florida*.

I wanted to be a pilot flying real aircrafts zealously and passionately. I was lucky enough to have parents who never stopped me from soaring high. On the contrary, they have always let me be myself. They had made daring decisions by gifting me my first battery-operated motorbike at the age of two and a real Harley Davidson when I was just Eighteen, not to forget a Doberman which I had petted for a couple of months. Daring and soaring high like an eagle were in my genes, and little can be done about inherited traits. Dad and Mom were okay with my decision to go to *Florida* to pursue a career in flying as a commercial pilot.

I was eager to start my flying course as soon as possible. I arrived in *Florida* on May 30, 2023, ready to embark on approximately a yearlong flying training. My goal was to become a commercial pilot, a profession that many found daunting, but I found exhilarating. Flying was not just something I wanted to do, but something I loved to do with all my heart. It was not a challenge, but a matter of joy.

I made beautiful memories in *Florida* during my brief stay at the flying school. I got to stay at a homestay a short distance away from my friends' house who I had met in *Bengaluru* while taking Ground Classes—*Raghav* and *Mayur*. We had all planned to join the same flying school, but they had arrived in *Florida* a couple of months before me.

The day I landed in *Florida* I first drove to the flying school where I had to complete some formalities.

After finishing the formalities, I took the school transport to go to *Raghav and Mayur's* house where we all partied till late in the night. It was quite a warm welcome.

I remember we had a ball of a time. I felt secure as now I had friends who would be like family. They were to be my friends, comrades, and mentors in the coming months. I was delighted to be in their company.

The next day, *Raghav* invited me to join him for a training flying sortie he was going to fly. I agreed without hesitation. We boarded a four-seater Cessna aircraft. *Raghav* and his instructor, who later became mine too, sat in the front seats. I squeezed into the back seat, which was quite cramped and uncomfortable. I didn't mind, though, as I was excited to witness some real flying on my first day at school. *Raghav* performed some crazy manoeuvres that made the plane spin and tilt in different directions. Him and his instructor seemed to enjoy it, but I felt sick. I would have loved it too if I hadn't partied hard and wasn't already jet-lagged. I told them I was feeling nauseous, but they didn't take me seriously. I jokingly threatened to vomit inside the plane, and they finally paid attention. They begged me to hold on for another fifteen minutes, but I couldn't control myself. I grabbed *Raghav's* bag and puked into it, as it was the only thing I could reach at that moment. He still hasn't forgiven me for that. He teases me about it every time we recall that incident.

Raghav was twenty-three years old and had studied International Relations at *Ashoka University* in *India.* He was a quiet and polite boy who spoke perfect English and had impeccable manners. Some of the other students at school and in our house made fun of him for that, but we were very close friends. He trusted me with his secrets, and we could talk about anything related to school and life.

Mayur was a more laid-back and fun-loving guy. He was also around the same age as *Raghav* and had a degree in Electrical Engineering. He and I got along well. Despite the age difference, we shared a sense of humour and laughed at our own silly jokes. He was also a great cook. He would whip up delicious dishes for us, which I am forever grateful for as I believe feeding somebody is truly a selfless job. Food was always a challenge in the US for Indians. I could barely cook anything except eggs.

I was assigned to a house that was cozy and comfortable, with many housemates. I got along well with everyone, but I had a special bond with *Diya*, *Carlos*, and *Christian*. *Christian* was a twenty-six-year-old *Colombian* who was four months ahead of me in the course. He was my aviation mentor and quizmaster. He would challenge me with questions on various topics related to flying and we would have lively discussions. He helped me prepare for the upcoming sessions at school.

Carlos was my partner-in-crime. He was about my age, and we had a blast together. We would do all kinds of crazy things at the homestay, much to the dismay and protest of the other housemates. But we didn't care, we were having too much fun. *Carlos* was from *Peru* and felt lonely because he was the only one from his country at the flying school. The Indians tended to stick together, so *Carlos* spent a lot of time in his room honing his knowledge as a pilot, though he was friendly with everyone. But we clicked instantly. We had no cultural barriers, just a shared sense of adventure and humour. We would spend a lot of money on weird stuff for the house, like mannequins, a Lightning McQueen bed from someone's trash, glow dolls, and Orbeez guns. We would fill the guns with water pellets and run around the house, playing spy games and annoying everyone else. We even bought an Xbox from eBay and got scammed. He still mourns the money he lost on that deal.

Diya had arrived at the flying school a month before me, but she hadn't started the course yet, as she was taking some classes. She was about my age and at the same level as me in the course, so it was easy to coordinate things with her. And as we did, our friendship grew stronger. We started out as convenience buddies. For the first month, I did everything on my own, like buying groceries, cooking food, cleaning, and other chores. But one day, I had an idea. I asked *Diya* if she wanted to split the cost of groceries and save some money as she was the other fellow Indian and our tastebuds were similar. She liked the idea and agreed. We also decided that she would cook, and I would clean. So, *Diya* and I continued with our deal without any problems. Later, when the deal worked out, we also rented a car together to go to school, as the school transport didn't offer us the flexibility of flying anytime. She didn't have an international driving license, but I did, so I drove her around. It was easier to sync our flying schedules that way. That made us even closer as friends. She was a kind and caring friend. She cooked good food.

And anybody kind enough to feed you is doing no less than gods' work. I think later she found joy in cooking what were once just meals enough to fill your stomach grew into her experimenting and trying her hand at South Indian dishes, *vada-pavs*[16] ,to India's famous butter chicken. They were my precious friends, and I will always cherish them and keep in touch with them.

I always had a passion for flying, and I was eager to learn from the best. That's why I joined a flying school in *Florida*, where I quickly became a student who was ahead of the batch. I don't mean to brag, but I had some advantages over my classmates. I had grown up with a love for machines, especially aircrafts. I had spent hours playing with mechanical toys, building models, and flying RC planes with my Dad. I had also flown at various RC flying grounds in Bengaluru, where I learned the basics of flying. So, when I came to *Florida*, I was ready to take on any challenge.

My instructor was a cool-headed guy from *Uruguay*, who always praised my skills. He said I had a natural talent for flying, and he taught me everything he knew. He was not a strict teacher, but a supportive mentor. He let me make mistakes and learn from them. He encouraged me to think creatively and handle any situation. Like they say, he allowed me to f*** around and find out. He was the best instructor I could ask for.

One of the most memorable moments of my training was my first solo flight. It was a big deal, because it meant I had earned the trust of my instructor and the school. It also meant I had to face a lot of pressure and expectations. Everyone was watching me as I took off and landed, performing various manoeuvres in the air. Some of my fellow students had told me horror stories of how nervous they were, how they messed up. But I was not afraid. I was confident and calm. I felt like I was born to fly. I followed the checklist, secured the cockpit, and took off smoothly. I enjoyed every minute of the flight, feeling the thrill of being in control. I landed perfectly, without a single bounce or skid. I had done it. I had completed my first solo flight, and it was awesome.

Everyone congratulated me and celebrated my achievement. My instructor was proud of me, and so was I. I had proven myself as a pilot, and I was one step closer to my dream. I had a lot more to learn and do, but I was ready for anything. Flying was not just a hobby or a career for me. It was my life. And I loved it.

As the tradition is at the flying school, after a successful solo flight, the T-shirt one is wearing is cut in a particular manner by the instructor, all your friends gather around you, congratulate you, pictures are clicked, and the moment is celebrated, turning it into a lifelong memory. I still remember every second of this ceremony. It was 12 July 2023. I had felt extremely happy as the moment was being celebrated. The instructor and all my friends wrote messages on the piece torn from the T-shirt. Pictures were clicked followed by a small party. They all rejoiced at my achievement. There were messages, short and sweet, from all my close friends present there but one message, though very simply worded, always caught my attention for some strange reason, inexplicable. It was from *Colonel Arun*. It read, "Sky is not the limit, keep soaring high." Later, when I was in the hospital, I knew what it meant. For me, it meant that just flying high in the sky is not the agenda, I will have to struggle to keep every ounce of my will, patience, and optimism alive to continue flying. Thanks Buddy.

It would be highly unfair if I do not give a special credit to my instructor who would just teach and coach in the most nonchalant way, giving me time and chances to mess up and straighten things out. He would not lead by holding our hands but let us fall, try again, and learn from our mistakes. This is what actual teaching is all about. It remains with you long after the lessons have ended. It prepares you for contingencies in life that come without warning. It teaches you to think out of the box to make things work, things that have fallen apart and look unmanageable.

Another unforgettable incident at the flying school was when I applied for my Private Check Ride[17]. This is when you get your private pilot licence. It is the progressive licence after the student licence, it was the personal licence I wanted to possess. A DPE-Designated Pilot Examiner from the FAA, the Federal Aviation Administration in *America*, conducts the flying exam. The first round is an oral exam. This is one of the most significant exams. It was more demanding and challenging than the solo flight.

The story is wild. The Check Ride Exam was at 6 A.M., and the school opened around 8 A.M. The school offers a room for the test to be conducted. The designated officer asked for the Maintenance record of the aircraft on which I had chosen to give the Check Ride, but the record was not available. He refused to proceed and was ready to go back. I pleaded with him to stay and called up the owner of the school. She somehow convinced him to stay on and continue with the test.

I did my part exceptionally well. The oral exam which was to be completed in half an hour was completed in just fifteen minutes by me. Then, the flight part began. To my utter astonishment, the officer started hurling insults at me and my entire family. He left no stone unturned to make me believe that I was a useless fellow who knew nothing about flying, and that my parents had wasted a fortune on me. For a little while, he succeeded in making me believe it. Fully convinced of failure in the exam, I landed the plane. But to my great surprise and relief, I heard him telling the school's owner that I had done a fantastic job, she was already present in the school after the whole ordeal. I had cleared it with an excellent grade and raving remarks from the officer.

The most hilarious part was that the exam was scheduled for one and a half hours, which I completed in just half an hour, so he had to wait to justify the minimum hours to legitimize the exam. He also congratulated me for the brilliant performance. He was kind enough to admit that it was a unique experience for him as well.

During my time as a student pilot, I encountered a memorable incident while navigating an uncontrolled airport. Unlike controlled airports with towers and ATCs directing aircraft, uncontrolled airports relied on a common frequency system. Pilots communicated their messages on this frequency, adhering to standardized procedures.

However, as part of my private training, I had to venture to a controlled airport and return to my uncontrolled base. This involved interacting with tower personnel, a daunting task for a student pilot with only 40 hours of flight time. My instructor accompanied me a few times, but eventually, I had to tackle it solo, under their endorsement.

The challenge was intensified by the VHF frequency distortion, featuring a diverse array of accents—American, Spanish, and Indian. Amidst the cacophony, I had to decipher instructions and maintain control of the aircraft simultaneously. Navigating unfamiliar airspace compounded the difficulty, especially judging runway dimensions that could deceive the eye.

My most challenging experience unfolded at Tamiami, an airport I had only visited once or twice. Despite the instructor›s reassurance, my attempts ended in multiple bounces during each landing—a humbling reminder of the complexities inherent in aviation. Though labelled a "good attempt", I left dissatisfied, recognizing the room for improvement in my skills.

I could not make peace with such a poor performance. I talked to *Raghav* whose father was a fighter pilot. He suggested that I try that all over again, all alone, and bump and bounce as much as I wanted. So, the next day, I did it again without my instructor, which was much more satisfying than the previous day's experience.

Now the next step was to get the Commercial Pilot licence. For this, one needs to have flown for a hundred or more hours, a concept called 'Time Building'. I was doing just that, that night, the fateful night.

Life in *Florida* was beautiful, like a melodious song, to be sung and enjoyed. It was a thrilling and satisfying song for a young teenager full of zeal and vigour. Everything was just at right place. Back in *India* my parents were happy with the way I was progressing. Here in *Florida*, I was content with the fact that I was doing justice to the money they were spending on me. I had a nice, comfortable, cozy life with my friends. Life was sorted. No struggle, all joy.

Life felt beautiful but never particularly courageous or persevering. In fact, it makes me laugh that today I see myself as 'brave and beautiful.' But now I have understood that being brave has nothing to do with having life all figured out or never questioning, wrestling, or struggling. Not at all. And beauty has nothing to do with perfection or an easy life. Being brave and beautiful means choosing to forge ahead. Choosing to show up on purpose, step by step, to help build a life or world we want to live in. Choosing to offer our light even when it feels like a tiny drop in a deep, wide ocean.

It means agreeing to become our true selves.

I read somewhere that all things that happen in your life happen for a reason, like me being born in a family that has a history of service. The life-changing incident that happened with me in *Florida* also happened for a reason. It was essential for me to explore my inner strength, my true worth. In fact, I feel more empowered now. I had not exploited my potential to the fullest even though I was doing pretty good among my batch mates. I had a knack for flying and it came naturally to me. I never had to struggle to understand, the understanding was just there. So, I never struggled a lot. Probably, that was why I had to struggle to really prove that I was totally prepared for the job I had dreamt to undertake. When you know more than others your test too, must be tougher than others. It was fair enough. Now I see the relevance of the whole incident in my life. Though it is easier said now than it was at the time I was suffering from the aftermath of the accident.

Overcoming obstacles is the only thing a pilot needs to learn after mastering the technicalities of flying an aircraft. Challenges are an integral part of a pilot's life. Challenges make life interesting. Overcoming them is what makes life meaningful. Obstacles are problems given to humans to solve. It could be something as big as being born with a disability or something as simple as learning how to ride a bike. The importance of overcoming obstacles in life is what needs to be taught in all institutions be it a family or a school. I can say proudly that I was prepared well by my family, and now I can say, by my school also.

Flight training isn't just about getting behind the controls of an aircraft. It also involves a significant amount of ground schoolwork. Student pilots must study subjects like aerodynamics, navigation, weather patterns, and aviation regulations. Balancing flight lessons with academic studies can be mentally demanding. Flying can be physically and mentally demanding. Student pilots often find themselves under a great deal of stress as they learn to handle various flight situations, from take offs and landings to emergency procedures. Maintaining focus and composure is crucial, and this can be challenging, particularly during the early stages of training.

When a student pilot hears tales of such problems by almost every student present or a pass out, it is natural to fear possible and predictable challenges. But it's more important to form a strategy to overcome your fears. It is all a mind game. The fear is in our minds and the strength to overcome the fear is also in the mind. This strength is what we call courage. Courage, just like any other virtue, is latent in every human being. We only need to ignite it when overcome with fear. A calm mind and positive spirit can lead you through adversities. So, love yourself. Value and respect your life. It is precious. It becomes valuable when you encounter death- face to face.

I have grown up hearing about the obstacles a pilot has to face. Becoming a pilot is a rewarding but challenging journey. Student pilots face financial, weather-related, academic, and time-related challenges. They must also cope with physical and mental stress, overcome plateaus in their performance, and navigate complex aviation regulations. Despite these hurdles, those who are passionate about flying and dedicated to their training can achieve their dream of becoming a certified pilot. The challenges they face during their training only serve to make them better, more capable aviators in the end. But the best lesson can be learnt when it comes unexpectedly. If it has happened to you during the training, then you have passed the toughest test. Defying the *Everglades* was the toughest test *Florida* could put me through. It was the longest test any pilot has ever been given. And I can proudly say that I have passed it with flying colours.

CHAPTER 3
THE FATEFUL DAY

| श्रेयान्स्वधर्मो विगुणः परधर्मात्स्वनुष्ठितात्"
"स्वधर्मे निधनं श्रेयः परधर्मो भयावहः ||[18]

(*It is better to perform one's own duty imperfectly than to perform another's duty perfectly. By doing one's prescribed duties, one attains spiritual growth; by performing another's duties, one incurs fear*)

The myth of *Icarus*[19] has always intrigued me as a student. It is taught that *Icarus* was too ambitious for his own good. He was warned by the master craftsman, his father, to fly safe, to go neither too high nor too low. If he flew high, the sun would melt his wings. And if he flew too low, the seawater would ruin the lift in his wings. Among multiple interpretations of the myth of *Icarus* and the *Daedalus*[20], I found the closest resemblance, in my case, was with that of narcissistic behaviour.

Honestly, many times we all fall too hard in love with ourselves, and this applies the most to teenagers. The 'grownup child' begins to believe that he is the best, the wisest, the most skilful and takes unreasonable decisions which later prove to be wrong, sometimes even fatal. This is the time the child needs hand holding the most. The most sensible, educated, and aware parents do it from behind, giving the impression to the adolescent that they are least interfering but are subtly guiding them and stand by them under all circumstances. And I am blessed to have a family that did just that.

The fateful day started like any other day with *Florida* heat. That day, during the day, *me* and *Diya* reached the flying school around eleven in the morning. Both of us had our flying slots booked. I had one slot from twelve to two in the afternoon, as a private pilot I have the privilege of flying alone anytime if the aircraft is free, I saw an aircraft free till twelve, hence to go to *Tamiami*, the airport that I feared once was now an airport that I could just go leisurely.

I completed the flight and came back home for lunch. I rested for some time and then joined my other housemates and their friends in the living room. They were discussing some Best Dressed Halloween Costume Competition to be held at school the next day, which was Halloween, 31 October 2023. The women in the house were all prepared to dress like Patrick Bateman from *American psycho* to *Greek goddess*, the men however were clueless and laughed at the lack of effort, I decided to at least put an honest effort, so *Diya* and I decided to go a nearby store for some last-minute preparation, nothing was satisfactory, so we returned home.

The whole city was beautifully decorated with hoardings for the various outlets luring people for Halloween parties.

The focus was more on the early morning slot for flying as our most important agenda was to complete the flying hours. The party arrangements could be made later.

Coming back to the events of the fateful day and resuming the story of my ambition which was simple, non-threatening and every bit achievable. I had shown my skills as a student pilot and obtained a Private Pilot licence. Like any other teenager, I wanted to earn and be financially independent. In my case, I was fortunate enough to be on path to achieve my goal quite early in life.

It was time now to get the Commercial Pilot licence so that I could become financially independent. But for this to happen, I had to pass couple of more tests and complete additional 100 more hours of flying by time building, i.e., simply borrowing an aircraft from the school for this purpose and fly to gain more experience. On that fateful day, I had set out to do just that. With the sole mission of being more skilled, proficient, and qualified to fly safely and efficiently. I chose to fly an aircraft at night, thinking that the flight would not be difficult. I had planned it well. I decided to go to the nearest airport for it.

I had one slot at night for time building and then again, an early morning slot from eight to ten the next day, so I decided to have a quick bite and rest for a little while. At around twelve in the night, I left for the flying school. Before leaving, I updated my logbooks and apps and messaged the details to all the relevant people as I did every time I embarked on a flight.

Boys generally don't talk to their parents as much as girls do. I have seen this in my family also. Studies have suggested that, on average, daughters tend to call their parents more often than sons, and mothers tend to receive more calls than fathers.

Some possible reasons for this gender specific may be firstly, because the daughters may have more emotional closeness and intimacy with their parents than sons and may use phone calls as a way of maintaining and expressing this bond.

Secondly, daughters may have more social expectations to fulfil the role of a caregiver and a communicator in the family and may feel more responsible for keeping in touch with their parents and providing them with emotional support.

Or mothers may have more influence and involvement in their children's lives than fathers and may initiate more contact and conversation with their children than fathers.

Or mothers may have more flexible and available schedules than fathers and may be more responsive and receptive to their children's calls than fathers.

However, these are not universal or absolute patterns. Therefore, it is important to consider the quality and meaning of the communication, not just the quantity, when evaluating the relationship between adult children and their parents.

This fateful day surely was unique or maybe the nature was giving some signals. Since it was night, I thought my must call my parents to tell them about my upcoming flight, as it was not very often possible to call them due to time zone difference. As it was daytime in *India*. I could connect with all three of them–Mom, Dad and *Fia*. *Fia* wanted to know what we were planning to do for Halloween, as the holiday is now gaining popularity in India as well. I told her that I would go to a friend's house, but nothing was decided. She was quite excited to know. Mom warned me against playing any spooky games like using a 'Ouija board' to try to contact the spirits of the dead. I laughed at her concern and assured her that I had no such plans. Dad was cool as usual and reminded me to be cautious. Assuming it was just like any other normal day and any other normal flight, I discussed the flight schedule with them and planned for the journey without the slightest hint of what fate had in store for me.

Everything went as planned. Dressed for the evening weather in a Shorts and T shirt, I boarded the aircraft assigned to me, a single-engine Cessna Skyhawk. I mentally checked all the details following the security checklist. Everything seemed perfect at that time. I took off from my home airport at around 01:00 AM and arrived at Okeechobee at around 02:00AM. I remember a sheriff car patrolling at the airport as I was taxing to the apron to park my aircraft, as I parked my aircraft shut off the engine got out his flashing lights were nowhere to be seen. The *Okeechobee* airport was virtually silent.

Lake *Okeechobee* covers 730 square miles and is remarkably shallow for a lake of its size, with an average depth of only 9 feet. The name *Okeechobee* comprises two words 'oki' which means 'water' and 'chobi' which means 'big' and was coined by the western Georgia Western tribe *Hitchiti*.

Lake *Okeechobee* is one of the largest freshwater lakes in the U.S., but the saddening part is that it is the most unsafe for swimming as it has toxic algae fed by agricultural fertilizers spread across the wide, shallow lake. It is also known that bull sharks and nearly 30,000 alligators live in this lake. It is the Gator Capital of *Florida*. Everglade Snail Kites, wading birds, waterfowl, Purple Gallinules, and myriad fish, frogs, and snakes, especially Burmese pythons, and turtles, rely on this sanctuary.

Taking off from Okeechobee, I checked the time on my watch. It was exactly 2:20 A.M. I was in the air, ecstatic at the freedom of the skies that kept me on cloud nine. The feeling of freedom was at its peak. It felt surreal to be high up in the air with total control of my aircraft and my life.

Even though everything seemed alright, I clearly remember that, somehow, I had a nagging doubt in my mind. I remember there was a time when I glanced at the altitude metre, and it showed 1700, so I noticed a drop in the altitude, and it panicked me. That was the moment when I realised something was off. But what was it? I kept flying. I had to keep going. I had to first figure out what was going on and then decide to control the aircraft. My mind raced. In a matter of seconds, I tried to understand what was happening. Was it some physiological effect of flying?

I knew very well that when you fly at night over water, you have zero references. Zero references mean that you have zero visibility and no landmark or sign to guide your route. So, there was nothing to see outside. I felt stupid. I could not comprehend what was happening. Was I hallucinating? I could not determine in which tilt position I was flying the plane, vertical or horizontal, whether I was climbing or descending, but I remember this happening. Then a cut. Had I misread the altitude? I felt like I had entered a cloud. There was zero visibility.

I looked at the instruments. They told me a different story, but my body showed some other signs. My body refused to align with the aircraft; at least, that was what I felt at that time. I, an experienced private pilot, could not make sense of this mismatch. I could not accept this at all. But it was a race against time. I had to figure out what was happening, and that was also very fast. When a disaster is imminent, a decision must be made quickly but wisely, with discretion.

I pushed myself. If the plane had tilted, my body would have felt the same thing, but it was not like that at that time. I was badly disoriented. It was all like a jigsaw puzzle. Nothing was making sense to me. And then, in a flash of a moment, it hit me that the movement was spiralling down. I had a quick look at the altitude-metre. It showed 300 or 250 feet. For a fraction of a second, I was stunned. A plane crash! Was it really happening? Was it really happening to me?

I remember military legend *Sam Manekshaw* who served for the Indo-British army and then became first field marshal of independent India famously said in one of his speeches, "if you must be bloody fool, be one quickly". I needed to decide whether to recover or ditch the aircraft in water, I had to think quickly. I decided to ditch the aircraft in water because I in my mind had thought, would I to recover, in the same black hole of sky which disoriented me and had made a fool out of me?

At that moment, it only occurred to me that I can't let the aircraft dip into the water. When pilots let that happen, they meet their end. When the mains of your aircraft touch the water at such speed your aircraft topples upside down like a toy. I remember, in my mind, I was counting six, five, four…this was the only time left with me. Precisely six seconds, not more than that.

And then, in a matter of seconds, the truth hit me. The plane had not crashed yet. But where was I? It was definitely not a cloud. I was about to hit the lake. The lake that had looked so enchantingly beautiful in the bright sunshine now looked ominous. Well, I knew for sure I had no time to think about it or regret my actions. What next? That was the critical question that occupied my mind. I quickly remembered the stories of crashes I had read about. Plane crashes in the *Everglades* were not uncommon. They happened all the time. But for a moment, a shiver ran down my spine; not a single pilot had ever survived any of those crashes. That was unsettling, rather terrifying. But it was a fleeting emotion. It vanished as quickly as it had appeared.

I was a lucky boy. I had survived the battle of life right at the time of my birth. I would live. My intuition told me–loud and clear. I would live.

I shall be the modern Icarus who would follow his intuition and would rely on everything that he possessed- his intellect and skill, his inherited genetic ability to act in times of adversities and his innate calm and composed nature. I could not have let down my grandfather and father who are warriors. Warriors do not give up until it ends.

But I had to figure out how. I did not have much time to spare, though. Think. I ordered myself.

I thought harder. I recalled that when the plane's tip touched the surface of the water, it felt like a solid wall because of the high speed. I had to stop the plane on the water's surface, not letting it slide on the lake's surface. I did just that. I did not let it sink or skid. I just gently parked it. I got stuck in the swamp but started to sink in it. I also knew that as soon as you stop your aircraft, it slows down and the water pushes it back. The aircraft can handle that, but the pilot's body is still flying at the same speed as before. It is like hitting a brick wall. I had to somehow manage to save myself from that massive jerk. How I did that, I still do not know.

Furthermore, I knew that the plane would not sink right away. Modern planes are designed to float on the water surface for some time to allow the crew and the passengers to escape. But the time was very limited. It would eventually sink as water filled up due to damage and uncontrolled landing. I was a blessed boy. I told myself again. I could make a safe landing. My intuition whispered to me again–ditch the aircraft deftly and you shall live.

I made a sincere attempt at what I thought as akin to ditching. There was an impact, and I could feel some gliding as I landed on the water. It must have happened in the right way despite the damage to the aircraft. The pilot had to dump the aircraft over the water just like a good skier. As soon as the main wheels touched the water, the water created so much drag that it could flip the plane but luckily it did not. As I hit the surface, the headlamp shattered due to the huge impact. I could not see anything inside the plane. I tried to look for the flashlight, but I could not find it. But I still breathed a sigh of relief that I had at least managed to control the aircraft and bought some time to plan my next move.

There was no time to celebrate, though. Feeling around in the darkness, I searched for the flashlight again but failed. Instead of wasting time, I chose to prioritize my future course of action. Another thing I had to do at the time of water landing was to open the doors and windows. It was the same as when your car falls into a large body of water and sinks; you cannot open them once it is fully submerged. I managed to open them from my side, seconds before landing.

Intuition is the whisper of the soul

CHAPTER 4
EVERGLADES: THE AERIAL LABYRINTH

शान्तात्मा विगतभीर्ब्रह्मचारिव्रते स्थितः ।
मनः संयम्य मच्चित्तो युक्त आसीत मत्परः ।।[21]

(Nature is not separate from the divine. When we surrender wholeheartedly to the supreme consciousness, we become one with the profound flow of existence. Just as river merges into the ocean, our souls find their eternal abode in the oneness of divine grace.)

In a world increasingly dominated by concrete jungles and digital distractions, the importance of nature in strengthening our soul cannot be overstated. When I sat atop the wing of my plane in isolation thinking about my friends, my family, and my childhood, I realised this fact that majorly 'overconfidence' and 'ambition' govern our lives. In this hurried world of "getting somewhere," we forget that nature is nurturing us, and, in return, we need to nurture it. After having spent almost nine hours among nature, I have concluded that learning about nature and finding ways to be an integral part of it should be taught to each child from an early age. Nature offers an alternative route to strengthen the soul, to fill it up with compassion and humility. It teaches us to expand our horizons: explore, learn, and grow but never "overdo". In doing so, not only do we evolve as individuals, but we are also able to share more gifts with each other. I realised that while thinking about all the people in my life, I remembered those who loved me. So, encountering nature reflects love and camaraderie.

Everglades are a beautiful place to explore. The expansive and mysterious *Everglades* are in the heart of *Florida*, where the land meets water with a delicate balance. It simply means a swampy grassland. A vast and unique ecosystem, the *Everglades* are a labyrinth of saw grass marshes, cypress swamps, and mangrove forests. It is a place of beauty and danger, where the line between earth and water blurs, and wildlife thrives. For pilots, navigating the *Everglades* is a challenge that requires skill, intuition, and a deep respect for the unpredictable forces of nature. That night was the first night when I had ventured out to explore the *Everglades* all alone.

I have enjoyed endless flights with *Raghav* over the *Everglades*. The more I flew over them, the more I found myself to be in love with the *Everglades*. To wander through the *Everglades* is to witness an old love story, one that spans the seasons and is never-ending. From the sky, I would look around and spot the tangled lily plants floating over the vast expanse, one with the water, barely showing the surface, I could feel my pure soul flow. I had often wanted to fly down, rest the plane on the vast waters and touch them, just touch them, and feel them. At this, *Raghav* would remind me of endless stories we heard about the challenges faced by commercial and student pilots in the *Everglades*. The stories seemed so real as if I had experienced them myself. *Raghav* being the son of a test pilot is a far more skilled pilot than me but even he found it challenging to fly over the *Everglades*. During the initial few flights, he would accompany me during the night flights as a private pilot even though they were my flights. He would come even at three in the night on his red scooter to pick me up. He would also keep narrating stories of pilots who faced unique problems while flying and we would give our own comments and opinions about them.

I had explored the wild beauty many times during the daytime and had diverse experiences there. After many short flights, I finally had an experience of seeing the wild side of the *Everglades*. I, now a seasoned private pilot with months of experience flying over diverse landscapes, had never faced a challenge quite like the *Everglades*. I had known myself to be of calm demeanour and steady hands, but even I felt a sense of trepidation, though momentarily, as I prepared to embark on a flight over this untamed wilderness for the first time after joining the flying school in *Florida*. The *Everglades* presented a unique set of challenges, from unpredictable weather patterns to the intricate network of waterways that crisscrossed the landscape.

I clearly remember the first day flight I had taken without *Raghav*. As I taxied my small plane onto the runway, I reviewed my flight plan meticulously. The *Everglades* were notorious for sudden changes in weather, and pilots had to be prepared for anything. The sky above was clear, but the *Everglades* had a reputation for conjuring storms seemingly out of nowhere. The challenge lay not only in flying through the narrow channels and open expanses but also in being vigilant for signs of impending weather changes.

As the plane ascended into the sky, I marvelled at the breathtaking expanse of the *Everglades* below. It was a sea of green, interrupted only by the sinuous paths of water winding their way through the marshes. From above, the *Everglades* looked like a living, breathing organism, teeming with life and energy. Yet, beneath this tranquil facade lurked the challenges that awaited any pilot daring to traverse this unique landscape.

As the flight progressed, I encountered the first hurdle – navigating through a dense network of water channels. The *Everglades'* labyrinthine waterways required precision and skill to navigate, as a wrong turn could lead to disaster. The landscape below seemed to shift and morph, making it challenging to maintain a steady course. Yet, my experience and keen instincts served me well as I skilfully guided the plane through the intricate maze.

The *Everglades,* however, had more in store for me. As I flew deeper into the heart of the wilderness, dark clouds gathered on the horizon, signalling an approaching storm. The *Everglades*, with their unpredictable weather, were living up to their reputation. I quickly adjusted my course, trying to outrun the storm that threatened to engulf my small plane.

The wind picked up, and rain lashed against the aircraft as I battled the elements. Lightning illuminated the darkening sky, revealing the treacherous terrain below. The *Everglades*, though stunning, could turn hostile in an instant. The challenge now was not just to navigate the waterways but to weather the storm and emerge on the other side unscathed.

With skill and determination, I guided my plane through the storm. The *Everglades*, true to its nature, tested me at every turn. Yet, as the storm subsided and the landscape below transformed once again into a serene expanse of green, I felt a sense of accomplishment.

Navigating the *Everglades* was indeed a pilot's challenge, but it was also a testament to the resilience and adaptability required to conquer the wild beauty of this unique ecosystem.

As the small plane soared above the *Everglades*, I couldn't help but marvel at the sheer majesty of the untamed wilderness below. The challenges faced were not just obstacles but lessons in humility and respect for the forces of nature. The *Everglades*, with their mysterious allure, had tested my mettle, leaving me with a profound appreciation for the delicate balance between man and the wild.

While we were coming back to the airport, defying the storm, and landing safely, I remember, *Raghav* had remarked that The *Everglades*, with their vast and intricate landscape, can be both mesmerising and perilous. He had waited for me holding his breath and was relieved to see me safe and sound. He had chuckled about what it would be like for a stranded pilot facing the challenge of surviving a night in this wild and untamed environment. I had replied nonchalantly that resourcefulness, adaptability, and a calm mind set are key to overcoming the myriad challenges that come with plane crashes.

I had no idea that the same wilderness would soon test me for a fiercer challenge and that also soon and that I would do all this to survive a plane crash. The only difference on that night was that my own aircraft turned hostile, and I was not given time to understand the matter. I can safely say that now I have experienced the beauty, as well as the dreadfulness of the *Everglades*.

We are taught at the flying school what happens as night falls over the *Everglades*, the priority for a stranded pilot is to assess the situation and prioritize basic needs. The pilot must take stock of available resources, starting with the aircraft itself. The plane can serve as a temporary shelter, providing some protection from the elements. The pilot should secure the perimeter of the aircraft, checking for any openings that may let in insects or small animals. In the *Everglades*, mosquitoes are not just a nuisance; they can be carriers of deadly diseases, making it crucial to minimize exposure. To ward off insects and provide some insulation against the cool night air, the pilot can use materials found in the aircraft, such as seat cushions or emergency blankets. These makeshift barriers can help create a more comfortable and secure sleeping area within the confines of the plane. I had learnt all this information by heart. But this experience taught me that bookish knowledge can never be applied directly. It taught me the difference between theory and practicality. My aircraft was full of water as the windshield had broken and the whole aircraft was submerged in water within minutes. I had to apply my presence of mind to get out of it well in time and use the articles within my reach in the best possible manner.

Moreover, navigating through the night in the *Everglades* requires not only physical preparation but also mental resilience. Darkness in the wilderness can be disorienting, and fear can become one's greatest enemy. To combat this, the pilot should use the aircraft's communication equipment to signal for help. Flares or distress signals may attract the attention of nearby search and rescue teams. Again, for me nothing worked. The network was so dim that the presence of my aircraft could not be detected. Remaining calm and focused is paramount during a survival situation. Creating a plan for the night, including designated rest periods and periods of vigilance, can help manage stress and anxiety. As a stranded pilot, I had to stay attuned to any changes in the environment, such as shifting winds or distant sounds, which may indicate approaching weather or other potential challenges.

Almost all student pilots at the flying school knew these facts about the *Everglades* by heart by the end of the term. One also gets to hear innumerable stories from students as well as experienced commercial pilots almost every day. Thus, nocturnal flight over the mesmerizing lakes of the *Everglades* is what I had decided to do to build the hours I needed for the Commercial Pilot licence. I was confident that since I knew everything I needed to know about this terrain, I was in a safe zone. Nature poses you a question that is uniquely framed for you, and you must write your own authentic answer. All my knowledge about the expected challenges came handy but I used it uniquely to suit my situation.

The stories of the happy crocodiles and alligators awaiting their prey and giant Burmese pythons gaping at humans with forked tongues, forever ready to devour them is what terrorizes stranded pilots. This is what I had understood from all the gory stories heard but they did not dissuade me even once. In fact, it never occurred to me that I would ever encounter them while flying. What was the connection between a pilot soaring high in the sky and these mute aquatic dwellers of the marshy lakes? And the possibility of a crash did not even cross my mind.

The funniest part is that all pilots are mentally prepared to face such a situation, but no one imagines even in their wildest of dreams that it would happen to them. It is supposed to happen to others, not to you. And this is where nature teaches you humility. The unpredictability of nature and of life is the same for all humans across the globe. It is a universal truth, undeniable. Nature catches you off guard and tests your physical, mental, and emotional toughness. And there cannot be any other place in the world that could be more notorious for this than the *Everglades*.

Despite the threat it poses to mankind, people visit this place in large numbers for adventure. Its popularity for adventure activities has not dwindled but increased many folds in the past decades so much so that it is now over exploited because of human activities. Hiking trails, kayaking, and canoeing, nature, and wildlife tours, biking trails, hiking and camping tours are some very common and immensely popular sports activities that attract tourists from all across the world. The activities are conducted under highly controlled conditions and no casualties have been reported. Mishaps are rare occurrences according to the reports. And this makes my experience even more unique. I got stranded at night and survived it all alone. My survival makes the *Everglades* unique for me! A challenge for the pilot which I have become.

I now firmly believe that Nature strengthens our soul. While sitting on top of the wing of the aircraft with nothing to do but experience the landscape I had time to ponder over so many ideas. Far away from the maddening chaos of everyday life, I realized that in the hustle and bustle of modern life, where technology and urbanization dominate our existence, the significance of nature often gets overshadowed. However, the profound connection between human beings and the natural world has been constant throughout history. With every flight, I explored newer ways in which nature nourishes and fortifies the human spirit, providing essential elements for our well-being.

One of the primary ways in which nature strengthens our soul is by offering a space for self-reflection and introspection. Amid towering trees, serene lakes, and rolling hills, individuals find a quietness that is rare in the urban cacophony. Nature serves as a canvas upon which we can paint our thoughts, unravel our emotions, and reconnect with our inner selves. This solitude allows for self-discovery, fostering a deeper understanding of our values, desires, and fears. In this way, the nine hours spent in the *Everglades* will remain etched in my mind.

When I had ventured out to explore the grotesque *Everglades*, I was in deep love with nature–day or night–it was equally beautiful for me. Even the eerie, threatening look it takes on had a peculiar beauty in it. I am yet to see if this picture of beauty would prevail for the rest of my life.

Extinction is the rule.
Survival is the exception.

CHAPTER 5
THE EYES IN THE SHADOWS

जातस्य हि ध्रुवो मृत्युर्ध्रुवं जन्म मृतस्य च।"
तस्मादपरिहार्येऽर्थे न त्वं शोचितुमर्हसि॥"[22]

(*This verse emphasizes that life is impermanent, and both birth and death are inevitable. Therefore, one should not grieve over what is bound to happen.*)

The moon hung low, casting a feeble glow over the murky *Everglades*. The air smelled of decay and dampness—the kind that clings to your skin, seeping into your bones. My Cessna lay mangled, its twisted metal groaning in protest. The crash had been brutal, jolting me awake from a nightmare of plummeting through darkness.

The water level inside the aircraft started rising quickly. Being a small aircraft, it started filling with swamp water faster than I had expected. I started feeling for my mobile which I remembered keeping next to me but could not find it. Without the headlamp and the flashlight, it was nowhere within my reach. At this time, I looked for any signs of hope. The front windshield had broken, so finally, I decided to squeeze out of the aircraft as the water reached my chin. I did not want to drown now.

This was one of those experiences that would leave a lasting mark on me for years to come. The plan was to free myself and squeeze out of the broken windshield and climb on top of the semi-submerged plane wings. I had to do it quickly. To free myself first I moved my left leg, and I could move it. I tried again; I could move a bit further and hoped for a quick escape from the plane's interior. I then tried pulling the right leg. But the right leg would not budge.

While I was caught in all this and trying to wriggle out my right leg, I sensed them—the *eyes in the shadows*. The gators. Their presence was palpable, primal. How did I know? Perhaps it was the sudden stillness—perhaps there was a sudden change in the vocalization in the way the 'cricket frogs' were calling, maybe it was their way of shunning attention but surely there seemed to be an eerie hush that settled over the swamp. Or maybe it was the way the moonlight danced on the water, revealing ripples that defied the gentle breeze.

The swamp's nocturnal symphony surrounded me—the distant croak of frogs, the rustle of unseen creatures, and the ominous hiss of the gators. I could feel and see it.

While I am a survivor and writing this post my recovery, the *Everglade* Gators definitely deserve a detailed mention in this memoir. The *Florida Everglades*—the very name conjures images of vast, murky wetlands, teeming with life. But beneath the tranquil surface lies a primal force—the American alligator. These reptilian giants, with their armoured hides and inscrutable eyes, are the true masters of this watery realm.

The alligator is more than a mere inhabitant of the *Everglades*; it is a keystone species. Its presence shapes the entire ecosystem. These ancient reptiles are architects, sculpting the landscape as they build nests and dig burrows. Their feeding habits—both gruesome and essential—maintain a delicate balance. They are nature's custodians, ensuring the health of this unique wilderness.

Alligators are ambush hunters. Patient and stealthy, they lie in wait, their eyes and nostrils barely breaking the water's surface. When prey approaches—a wading bird, a fish, or even a small mammal—the alligator strikes. Its powerful jaws snap shut, propelled by muscles that can generate over 2,000 pounds of pressure per square inch. Bones shatter, and death is swift.

Make no mistake: alligators are quick when exiting the water to attack their prey, their initial burst of speed is their deadliest weapon—a surprise assault that catches victims off guard. Once they've secured their meal, they retreat to the water, where they feast in relative safety.

Despite their fearsome reputation, alligators rarely pose a threat to humans. Most attacks occur due to illegal feeding, which emboldens the animals. When humans become part of their food chain, the alligators lose their natural fear and may strike rather than flee. So, remember respect their space, and they'll respect yours.

I am sure a basic question which will be going around everyone's mind is, Will an alligator eat a human? The answer is complex. Alligators primarily feed on fish, birds, and smaller mammals. However, if provoked or cornered, they won't hesitate to defend themselves. Fatal attacks are exceedingly rare—just one in 3.2 million. Yet, the *Everglades* echoes with tales of those who ventured too close, who ignored the boundary between curiosity and danger.

The water quickly started filling up, something slimy touched felt my body. My mind raced. I couldn't die here—not like this. The adrenaline surged, and I did the unthinkable. With trembling hands, I reached for my right leg. The pain was blinding as I tore through flesh and sinew. My heel hung by a thread, and the calf muscles spilled out like raw meat. I twisted, wriggling like a worm. Pain shot through my leg, and I bit my lip to stifle a scream. But it was a small price to pay for survival.

Blood mingled with the swamp water, and I fought to keep my head above the surface. But I knew I couldn't stay here. The unthinkable would find a way—its primal hunger driving it forward.

I glanced upward. The plane's wing jutted out, few feet above the waterline. It was my only chance. Summoning every ounce of strength, I squeezed myself through the broken windshield. There were countless cuts which I would be healing later but, in that instant, I pulled myself up. My severely torn leg protested, but I ignored the pain. I scrambled onto the wing, my heart pounding.

The ordeal was not over for me, In the desperation of freeing my leg and excruciating pain, I was not able to get my backpack from the aircraft which had my passport, I had thought I'd deal with that later. I had to again go down into the cabin of the aircraft to search for my phone, iPad and my bag.

It was moonlit and I had to do everything in this light. I slowly lowered my legs into the nose of the plane and when I didn't feel any movement, I went into the cabin I tried feeling for the phone, iPad, or any other useful item. The backpack was floating, and I could get hold of it in the first instance only. I kept feeling the floor of the plane with my hands and feet. This adventure of mine was thwarted the moment I felt something sliding past me. I had heard about *Everglades* being infested with pythons and it sliding force felt like a large reptile.

Having just got a temporary relief from the gators I didn't want to get into newer adventures. I immediately squeezed back on to the nose and climber the wing of the plane.

While I was extricating now, in addition to getting my bag, which had not only my passport and other essential documents but also one snicker in it, I also decided to pull out two red cushions from the seat of the aircraft, these cushions not only serve as floating devices. I thought, if necessary, they would also come in handy to signal the rescue team as they were bright red in colour.

Once atop again, for hours, I clung to that wing, my torn leg throbbing. and the swamp came alive with the sounds of waking creatures.

But I wasn't done. Survival wasn't just about escaping their jaws—it was about surviving the night with the severe wound and being discovered and rescued before falling prey to the injury or the predator.

My wound bled freely, and the heel had been dangling for some time. I had to stop the bleeding. The only thing that I could think at that time was my T shirt only piece of cloth on my upper body. But these synthetic cloths are quite strong it is difficult to tear them, then I remember having the I card along with the pen in my neck. I used the pen to puncture a hole in the T shirt and then I tore a strip of cloth from my shirt, tying it tightly around my leg.

Once on top of the plane, sitting on the wing, I could see the planes flying in the sky, but they were too high. Initially, I tried to catch their attention by waving the cushion and screaming but gave up soon. They could neither see me nor the cushions, so I decided to save my energy for the right moment and stopped trying.

Out on the plane, I realized that a cool sea breeze had started blowing with great force, making it very cold. I thought I would freeze to death, but sooner than I expected, it turned out to be numbing; no sensation at all, no feeling of cold or warmth, just neutral. For an hour, I adjusted the cushion to block the breeze coming from behind my back. Thankfully, the breeze was blowing only in one direction and not from all sides. I sat in that same position for an hour and felt that my body and brain had gone into hibernation. No sensation at all, neither physical nor emotional. It was a matter of sheer survival. The body and mind worked together. But I had to survive at any cost. I was drifting into nothingness, and I had to stop and reverse it.

I distracted myself. I asked myself a thousand questions or perhaps the same question in a thousand different ways.

Was it wise to fly at night? I knew very well about the dangers lurking in the *Everglades*. Then, what prompted me to take this decision?

Why did no one stop me from doing it? My school authorities, friends, parents–no one stopped or warned me.

What does it indicate?

Of course, it was an ordinary thing to fly airplanes at night over the *Everglades*. I could still see so many flying over me.

I am not an Icarus in this manner. I have not ignored any warning or defied any rule. Then why is Icarus haunting me? It was probably my overconfidence that landed me here.

Or was it some fault in the aircraft? How could the plane come spiraling down in a jiffy, without any warning? But accidents do not warn before happening. If they did, they wouldn't be called accidents.

All these questions bothered me for quite some time, and I tried to find answers to them. It was the survival mechanism of the mind. The mind had to accept the reality that I was in a messy situation. And I could not reverse it. The quicker you accept the contingency, the better it is.

Acceptance largely reduces fear. Having accepted the accident and the fact that I was stranded in the middle of nowhere, in the dead of night, brought me face to face with reality. I had planned to spend Halloween back home with my friends, who were all planning to watch a scary movie with me and enjoy without knowing here I was fighting the battle for my life. I was not aware what the night had in store for me. Whether I will be able to see the light of the day, or the *Everglades* will engulf my plane and I will become a feed for the gators. They would have no clue where I was or what I was going through. I missed them all.

The idea of elves, fairies and zombies was soon replaced by the thoughts of alligators, crocodiles, and pythons. Another fear I had to overcome if I had to be a modern Icarus. I could not let myself be a victim of my fate. It was a planned venture, so I had to plan my survival. I just made a silent prayer to God not to laugh at me this time. Just this time.

But I was alive. The creatures slithered away, defeated—for now.

CHAPTER 6
A NIGHT IN THE EVERGLADES

या निशा सर्वभूतानां तस्यां जागर्ति संयमी|
यस्यां जाग्रति भूतानि सा निशा पश्यतो मुने: ||[23]

(Perception of light and darkness can be relative. Just as the night seems dark to most, the enlightened sage perceives it as a time of introspection and inner illumination. So, indeed, after every dark night, there is a brighter day waiting for those who seek wisdom.)

The survival mantra for me was indeed resilience, optimism, and belief that I would find a way to survive despite the darkness, both literal and metamorphic. For me this proverb turned out to be true in both ways. Literally speaking, my hope was founded on the fact that help would arrive soon after dawn. Metaphorically, this episode is like a dark night which has ended and has left me in bright sunlight. I feel enlightened about many aspects of my personality which I would not have known had this not happened to me.

***

This age-old adage encapsulates a profound truth that resonates across cultures and time periods. It symbolizes hope, resilience, and the inevitability of positive outcomes following challenging times. While writing my story, I explored the multifaceted dimensions of this proverb, delving into its psychological, philosophical, and practical implications. Through an examination of real-life examples, historical events, and psychological theories, I could unveil the resilience inherent in the human spirit and the transformative power of adversity. This revelation has also prompted me to write this story. It has made this gory experience a meaningful one for me.

In the absence of the above three, the darkness of adversity will engulf the victim. Life, by its very nature, is a series of ebbs and flows. Adversity is an intrinsic part of the human experience, manifesting in various forms such as personal struggles, societal challenges, or global crises. These dark nights, whether they be individual or collective, test the limits of our strength and resilience. Yet, embedded in the fabric of this darkness is the promise of a new dawn.

So, it was very natural for me to ask myself, “What pulled me through that night?” Definitely, my resilience. But what does it really mean? It is nothing but a mind game. Resilience, defined as the ability to bounce back from adversity, is a psychological strength that allows individuals to endure hardships and emerge stronger. The darkness of the night becomes a crucible in which resilience is forged, transforming individuals into more robust versions of themselves.

Let me explain. When I realized that there was no light inside the aircraft because the headlights had broken and I could neither find the flashlight or my phone, and when I felt the gator closing in, I became determined to survive. I acted in the faint moonlight which was just enough to grope for things. At that time, there was no such realization of resilience. It was inherent, honed right from my childhood. At that time, my mind worked as it was trained to be, with calmness and with an urgency demanded by the situation. The promptness with which I acted, despite the physical injury, underlined the fact that I was in trouble which needed more effort than usual, and it was my natural demeanour to act like that. When faced with adversity, individuals often engage in re-framing negative situations and finding new perspectives. This flexibility allows them to perceive the potential for growth and positive change, even amid challenging circumstances. My mind was guiding me to do the same.

Sitting on the wing of the aircraft, I recalled numerous instances from history of how mankind has survived both natural and man-made catastrophes. Throughout history, there have been numerous instances where societies and individuals faced seemingly insurmountable challenges only to emerge from the darkness with newfound strength and resilience. Survival is not just about enduring but about thriving in the face of adversity I recalled Winston Churchill's iconic speech during World War II, which I had learnt about it in school. "...**We shall fight on the beaches, we shall fight on the landing grounds, we shall fight in the fields and in the streets, we shall fight in the hills; we shall never surrender**." The *Everglades* swamp were now my landing grounds and my beaches, I couldn't surrender, how could I? when these men didn't.

On an individual level, the life of *Helen Keller* serves as a testament to the triumph of the human spirit over adversity. Deprived of both sight and hearing from a young age, *Kell*er faced immense challenges. However, with the guidance of her teacher, *Anne Sullivan*, *Keller* not only learned to communicate but went on to become a prolific author and social activist. Her life exemplifies how personal darkness can be dispelled by the sunlight of determination and resilience.

I was thankful that I had all my senses intact. I recalled what my instructor had taught us at the flying school. He had always made us struggle, bounce and bump and go wrong and then insist on doing things the right way ourselves. I knew what he was aiming to teach but now I have understood the importance of letting the student explore and experience on his own. I was entirely on my own. He was my *Anne Sullivan.*

Nature befriends those who face them with courage and consumes those who turn timid and weak. I was the strong breed.

In Western philosophy, existentialism acknowledges the inevitability of human suffering but posits that individuals have the power to create meaning in their lives. Existentialist thinkers like Viktor Frankl, who survived the horrors of the Holocaust, argue that even in the darkest moments, individuals can find purpose and meaning. Frankl's concept of finding meaning in suffering underscores the transformative potential of navigating through the darkest nights. This is where I found meaning in my predicament. The questions, “Why me?” or “What sin have I committed?” become meaningless. Difficulty, pain and grief are inevitable in human life. I was quite surprised at myself that this horrifying experience did not make me give up my dream to become a pilot. In fact, I believe that this experience has honed my skills further.

This was indeed the longest night I had ever spent in isolation, severed from human civilization. The pitch darkness around me was simply unending. Danger could have lurked from any side. One moment of daze and my story on this earth would be over. One look at the waters of the lake showed me what could be my future abode if I ended up making a little mistake.

I recalled the tale of a drowned pilot whose plane had crashed into the deadly *Everglades*. The pictures of his half-found body haunted me. His pants were found with some remnants of his legs. I could only imagine seeing the body floating in the lake right in front of me. He had become a sumptuous meal to a ferocious alligator. At one point, I am sure, I saw my body in the same pants floating in the lake right in front of my aircraft. I felt beads of sweat on my forehead. I shrugged the thought aside. I did not want to nurture such thoughts at all. I was determined to pull through the deadly, bitter, and cold night and with the first ray of sunshine, the rescue team would locate me, and I would reunite with my friends.

This is what kept me going and jolted me back to reality. I was now shivering, and my foot felt warm. But I was not inclined to pay any attention to the dangling ankle of the left foot. For once in life, I was glad to feel the pain. I could not afford to go into a state of hibernation and meet a fatal end. I will not give others the satisfaction of creating tales of one more pilot who met a pathetic end in the *Everglades*. With these daunting thoughts I kept my hope alive. Optimism was what I had inherited in abundance from my family.

The night was becoming darker, fiercer, colder, threatening and engulfing. I felt like an embryo in a mother's womb. The night was the womb, and I was all alone, crouching to hold on to life, in my most rudimentary form, at the mercy of nature. At the same time, there was a sense of security that I felt. It was as shocking as it was confusing. Despite my ebbing physical strength, I was gathering strength from the ferocious nature. My mother's intuition had saved me from dying an untimely death. I was hopeful that this night would also save me from the dangers lurking. I was sure the night would sustain me and not let my youth go to waste. I had to be resilient, patient, and sane. If I managed to let my sanity prevail till dawn, I would succeed.

It is fascinating to contemplate the scene now in retrospection. The human experience is rife with paradoxes, and few are as poignant and metaphorically rich as the dual nature of the mother's womb and the predicament of a pilot stranded in a lake in the middle of the night. On the surface, these two scenarios seem worlds apart—one symbolizing the epitome of safety and nurturing, the other representing a situation fraught with danger and isolation. However, upon closer examination, a profound analogy emerges, revealing the intricate interplay of threat and safety and vulnerability. However, there are threats lurking in the shadows. The very womb that nurtures life can also become a source of threat. Genetic abnormalities, complications during pregnancy, or infections can jeopardize the well-being of the unborn child. The safety of the womb, paradoxically, becomes the crucible of potential danger. This duality reflects the complexity of life, where vulnerability and resilience coexist in an intricate dance. The plane was stuck securely in the marshy lake but amidst life threatening aquatic fauna. A paradox indeed! However, akin to the paradox inherent in the mother's womb, this perilous situation also unveiled my potential for resilience and survival.

The isolation in the abyss of darkness can be threatening not only physically but also psychologically, but, surprisingly, it was not the fear of the unknown, but the known. Pilots who had lost their lives must have feared the facts they knew to be true and lost their cool. My mind told me that I knew what was expected under the exceptionally still water. So, if I knew what lay underneath then why be scared? This gave me strength for now I only had to form a strategy for survival and that also till the dawn. Magically, the moment I had this thought, half the battle had already been won. Now, the deep dark night and the stillness around did not make me feel insecure.

My conscious mind was my guiding light. Despite the isolation and uncertainty, I could think somewhat clearly what the solution to my problem could be. I had to find a way to survive through resourcefulness, adaptability, and sheer determination. The wisdom to unravel the analogical paradox can come only in a condition of extreme adversity. For me, it was extreme adversity. In that state of isolation and peacefulness, I had to find security in the darkness and defy nature. The cognizance of these seemingly disparate experiences converging to illuminate the complexity of the human condition, where dualities coexist in a delicate balance, has matured me in an inexplicable manner. Both the embrace of safety or the throes of threat ultimately convey that the capacity for resilience resides within each individual but needs to be honed during one's growing years, which later transcends the specifics of their circumstances.

The *Everglades*, with their vast expanse of marshes, water channels, and dense vegetation, can be a disorienting and hauntingly beautiful place even under normal circumstances. However, when pilots find themselves stranded in this wilderness, atop a partially submerged plane in the stillness of the night, the mind can play tricks on them. Another psychological battle. Hallucinations, fueled by exhaustion, stress, and the eerie surroundings, became a surreal companion to the already challenging situation.

I imagined myself to be in my grandparent's house in India's Punjab enjoying the winter vacation. The lazy days spent at their house, pampered by Grandma and Grandpa with delectable delicacies served in the room, at times, against my parents' wishes. The cozy house, the cozy bedroom, the cozy bed, and the warm comforter, this is where I imagined myself to be. What a blissful experience!

The top of the aeroplane was feeling warm and comforting just with these memories. I was in a dream, a beautiful dream. This must have been a coping mechanism of my mind.

Next, I remembered *Diya's* 'blankie', the nice plush and soft blanket we both used to fight to wear at night. The ownership of the blanket was a perpetual bone of contention between us. She would get terribly irritated as I bullied her into sharing her blanket with me. So many times, she had pulled it off me after coming back from the flying school and discovering that it was with me. Alone and abandoned in the bitter cold I found solace in imagining myself to be in it. The red cushions were no less than the blankie at that moment. The wind was blowing from behind me, and the cushions were protecting me from the cold sea breeze. I was in an imaginary world.

I did not want to drift into sleep as my body may have given up due to fatigue but the survival instinct kept me going. I looked around. Nature is dramatic. It conveys without speaking.

The saw grass surrounding the crash site took on exaggerated forms, casting elongated and distorted shadows. The subtle movements of the vegetation in the night breeze seemed to morph into ethereal shapes, dancing at the edge of my peripheral vision. As I was already fatigued from the crash and the subsequent struggle for survival, I felt a twinge of disorientation. This could prove fatal. I could not afford to wink my eyes. I had to remain awake despite the hallucinations. Every little ripple in the waters would make me skip a heartbeat, not because of fear but out of caution. This was another coping strategy of the cautious mind.

Sitting atop the wreckage of the plane, marooned in the heart of the ***Everglades***, the once vibrant landscape now seemed like an alien realm, draped in the oppressive silence of isolation. The once familiar domain in bright light was now unrecognizable. The realization of my predicament settled in with every passing second and a creeping unease began to take root in my mind. The constant struggle between the lurking death and my superb will power to survive was becoming exhaustive. I could give up any moment. My body yearned to stretch and relax, my mind was screaming for a nap and my instinct urged me to curb both. Thankfully, both my mind and body cooperated. Yet again, this was the result of the defence tactic my body and brain were getting accustomed to.

One moment I would hallucinate an incident from my childhood and the next moment I would see eerie creatures from the surroundings stare at me. I recalled the slimy creature that had brushed past my foot when the plane had ditched, and water had crept in. My instinct told me that it was a small creature but a monster like creature could attack any moment. I was jolted out of my present state of dizziness. I had to be practical. It was not so difficult. I only needed to survive till the morning. I made some rough calculations. Within about three to four hours, it would be morning and I would be rescued! I had to survive till then and not attract attention from the creatures inhabiting the swamp.

The stillness of the night, punctuated only by the occasional croak of unseen frogs, became an ominous backdrop to my mental ordeal. My senses would be on high alert, and every rustle in the underbrush or ripple in the water made me more cautious, and with equal speed subside, and make me lethargic. My gaze fixated on the water, searching for any sign of movement. The *Everglades*, with its reputation for housing alligators and other dangerous aquatic creatures, became a breeding ground for my anxious thoughts. Every subtle ripple became a potential threat, and the absence of visible danger only fueled my imagination, creating a mental landscape teeming with unseen eyes.

The never-ending night and the endless stretch of darkness enhanced my sense of helplessness and frustration. Will this ever end? I tried to distract myself. I thought about Carlos. The time when he had been duped of one thousand dollars shopping online. I imagined having a gala time with him in his house playing on the X box that had never arrived. The loud snickering that disturbed everyone else in the house, but we did not care a bit.

The night in the *Everglades* was not silent, but rather, it was a symphony of sounds that evoked both fascination and dread. The distant calls of birds, once a comforting melody, now carried an unsettling tone. The nocturnal chorus of frogs, a familiar background noise in the *Everglades*, now seemed to communicate in a secret language that only intensified my sense of isolation. The unseen creatures, hidden in the darkness, became collaborators in an unnerving performance. Their calls, once harmonious, now resonated with a haunting quality that echoed in the recesses of my mind. Were they all conspiring against me? I would tell myself, "No, they are making a call to the universe to save me."

Yes, they were. They were telling the universe that I was trapped there, one poor nature lover who meant no threat to the environment but was a victim himself. They were my well-wishers, and they were conveying the message to my well-wishers in the other world, my friends and family. I had to gather every ounce of my will power to stay still and be patient.

My friends would be watching a horror movie about zombies. And here I was amidst water, once a potential source of survival, now a symbol of impending danger. I, an adventurous young adult of nineteen years, an animal lover, was imagining the possibility of being dragged and torn apart to pieces brutally by an aquatic beast. How would this be picturized? My subconscious mind was being playful even at this time of disaster. I was the hero of my movie. Perseverance, courage, and faith will pull you through, my dear son, my mind would say. And I believed it.

The most astonishing and commendable feature was that I was not afraid, even for a fraction of a second. I remember, I had laughed loudly, when I was shaken up with fear and even gestured frantically to brush aside an imaginary wild creature which was just a shadow of an aircraft in the sky. The dim moonlight and the crazy ideas in my mind made me believe momentarily that I was being attacked and out of reflex action I tried to wade it away. Upon realizing the truth, I laughed at it. This changed my mood.

Another realization! Nature, even in its most gory form, can change your mood. I went down memory lane. So many times, in my childhood I would silently go to the park or in the wilderness to change my sulking mood when I unhappy on being denied something or when I was being troubled. Any kind of contact with nature makes you tranquil and distracts you from trouble. Many times, it will even provide you with a solution to your troubles.

As the night wore on, the *Everglades* revealed another layer of their mystique. The most fascinating and unforgettable experience. Fireflies, tiny bio-luminescent creatures, emerged from the vegetation, creating a dance of lights that added to the surreal atmosphere. This enchanting display became a source of entertainment. Did I see a rhythm in their dance? Did I see that the steps were beautifully synchronized? I am not sure, but it was entertaining. Something I enjoyed. The fireflies truly are a symbol of the *Everglades*' nocturnal beauty.

I yearned for the sun's rays to pierce through the shadows, dispelling the illusions that were haunting me through the night. The mental trauma of isolation, exacerbated by the imagined dangers of the *Everglades*, reached its zenith as I clung to the hope that daylight would bring clarity and rescue. My prayers had to be answered. There was no way I was leaving this world without reuniting with my family. I made one earnest prayer to all the entities surrounding me to spare me and protect me and clear my path of freedom. I thanked the leaves, the grass, the frogs, the fireflies for being around. I befriended them to be my guardian angels and make me see the dawn.

Instantly, I saw a faint ray of sunlight and it was no less than a miracle, as if the guardian angels had made the sun rise on my humble request. It must have been almost four hours since I had landed the plane on the lake. I still wasn't sure if I was hallucinating or was it time for daybreak, but I could no longer endure the darkness. Here my patience had begun to fade, there, the darkness had started to fade. The *Everglades*, in their nocturnal symphony, became both a companion and a threat, a reminder of the delicate balance between man and nature. I learnt a valuable lesson of never underestimating nature.

I felt a strange transformation as if something inside me had changed drastically. I was not the same person who had been flying an aircraft with immense zeal and zest with no apprehensions about the mundane things in life. I felt extraordinary and exclusive, calm, and composed, humbler for I had felt so petty in front of the vastness of nature. The immense power it has upon us.

The night had been transformational. It made me love and respect life. I realized the insignificance of man in front of nature.

"God uses rescued people to rescue people."

CHAPTER 7
THE DAWN OF RESCUE

ज्योतिषामपि तज्ज्योतिस्तमसः परमुच्यते |
ज्ञानं ज्ञेयं ज्ञानगम्यं हृदि सर्वस्य विष्ठितम् ||[24]

(*Hope is not merely wishful thinking; it is the ability to perceive light even when surrounded by darkness. Just as the sun rises after the darkest night, our inner light—the knowledge and wisdom—shines forth, guiding us through life's challenges.*)

This profound statement suggests that even in the darkest moments, the human spirit has the capacity to perceive a glimmer of light, a source of encouragement that can guide individuals through their struggles. Hope and positivity simply mean illuminating the darkness. Hope is all a game of the mind. It is a belief that despite challenges and setbacks, one can fight through difficulties and achieve a better tomorrow. In this sense, hope serves as a mental roadmap, guiding individuals through the darkness by providing them with a sense of direction and purpose. In times of adversity, the human mind often tends to focus on the negative aspects of a situation. Hope, however, acts as a counterbalance, allowing individuals to shift their perspective and envision a positive future. It empowers individuals to confront challenges with a proactive mindset and this is the survival instinct which humans have developed. Focusing on positive aspects such as finding food, shelter, and safety enhances our chances of survival. Negativity, on the other hand, can lead to stress and hinder decision making. Positivity provides us with the emotional strength needed to withstand the storms of life, fostering a sense of inner peace and stability.

***

It was a long night; winters in *Florida* sounds like an oxymoron, but hear it from me, someone who is injured and wet from head to toe and bare body in just shorts, in the pitch darkness of night with predators eyeing you from the shadows, it feels unbearable. All I wanted at that time was the night to set and Sun to show up. At this time, I realized why so many cultures worship the Sun.

Across various cultures and religions throughout history, Sun worship holds profound significance. The Sun, essential for life on Earth, provides light, heat, and energy. Symbolizing power, vitality, and illumination, its daily rise and fall mirror cycles of birth, death, and rebirth. Many cultures personify the Sun as a deity—such as *Ra* in ancient Egypt, *Helios* in ancient Greece, *Surya* in Hinduism, and *Inti* in Incan religion. Sun worship often aligns with solstices and equinoxes, marking celestial transitions with deep spiritual meaning.

As the energy source behind photosynthesis in plants and the foundation of the food chain, the Sun's cultural context varies, reflecting local beliefs and practices. Beyond mere physical properties, it embodies both life and spirituality!

The hope that I had kept alive all through the grotesque night was rewarded with the first ray of sunlight.

As dawn broke over the *Everglades*, the gators retreated to their lairs. They vanished into the reeds, leaving ripples in their wake. Their legacy endures—their ancient lineage a testament to survival. So, when you visit this wild expanse, remember the alligators. They are the guardians of a primordial world, where danger and beauty coexist in murky harmony.

I could not have done anything but wait till the Sun would shine, which was finally at 7:09 A.M, time of actual twilight on 31 October 2023, as I checked later. I felt utterly helpless as I was not aware if there was someone searching for me and if my plane's tracking system is sending out any coordinates.

My phone could not be traced and, all in all, I had been totally cut off from human connection for around five hours since the crash. The hope of being rescued after the daybreak had got me through the night. The first ray of Sun brought a glimmer of life. My way to freedom. And the reality of my surroundings and circumstances became clearer. The darkness and stillness of the night had completely confounded my senses and judgement.

When I looked around the swamp lake, I saw a shoal of fishes trying to nibble into patches of reddish something in the marshy water. I clearly remember it was blood red. That was my moment of awakening. The wound in the right leg caught my attention. It was my blood which was leading the fishes to sanguinary, that had flown in abundance into the lake water. I had felt no pain in my leg till that time. But when I looked at my right leg, I was far more than horrified.

I had to touch my leg to keep feeling if it was still there, I was sure by the time, and if ever, I am evacuated, my right leg would have to be amputated, but at that point of time it was not my biggest worry, the adrenaline was still rushing and a scream got muffled in my throat because my body and feelings were still in survival mode and were not reacting yet. But the sight of the blood still oozing out jerked me out of my little daze.

At night when I tore my T shirt to somehow keep the ankle of the right leg which was dangling like a ping-pong ball on one side and, along with that, a huge piece of mass from the calf muscle was hanging out baring the bone in the leg, however, with first light I could see I didn't do a decent job and now didn't have anything else on me to do further bandage. Anyone would have fainted at that sight. The feeling of helplessness had reached its peak. Here, I was staring around, right in the middle of wilderness, totally helpless, without any medicine, tools, or equipment to tend to it any more than I had. The lack of any knowledge of first aid required to be given horrified me. But I had grown up immensely overnight. I took deep breaths and pondered over the situation. What could I do? With a little thinking, I knew what needed to be done. Without losing my calm, I searched for the Swiss knife I always keep with me for emergency situations. I picked up the bag and searched thoroughly for it. There was no sign of it though, it had probably jerked out and fell inside the aircraft when I had crash landed on the swamp. So, now when I needed it the most, I could not locate it.

I looked around. The surroundings looked less ghostly, rather pleasing in the morning sunlight. I looked down into the water and saw an ugly black dumb fish. How could a fish be so ugly? Talking about ugly fishes, the *Psychrolutes Marcidus*, or the smooth-head blobfish is known to be the ugliest fish, but I rather find them cute.

Okay maybe not cute, but 'ugly-cute' as there is a very thin line between being cute and ugly.

I was amused at my own thoughts. My humour was still alive. I could see the funny side of the poor little fish! Hailing from military family I have heard countless stories of men in battle, ready to give it their all, men facing certain death at times like this humour is a morale booster for these men. I in no way stand in the same pedestal as these men but it was a good sign indeed.

I examined the water once more. It was strangely still. It was layered with lilies; these swamp lilies have a green colour on top and a red-purple hue on the bottom. The water was covered with these plants and a little movement was also conspicuous to the human eye. I saw some movement. I am sure I saw a weird brown creature wriggling under the leaves and camouflaging against the apparently tender stems of the lily plants. Straining my eyes further, it turned out to be a python, most probably the Burmese Python, which is I believe is notorious for causing havoc with the *Everglades*' delicate ecosystem, leading to sever declines in native wildlife sightings, in response to which *Florida* has eased hunting regulations, allowing the removal of these invasive reptiles to protect the ecosystem of the swamp. The python was as thick as double the diameter of my arm. Now that was alarming.

A lot of blood had oozed out into the water, attracting little fish and other aquatic animals, I was fearing if the metallic smell of my blood would be encouraging the alligators and crocodiles to lick their lips in predatory anticipation. Having survived through the night, I did not want to be again attacked by a predator in broad daylight. The flora and fauna of the ecosystem that seemed bearable and rather attractive now in the bright sunshine had given me the most intriguing time of my life the night before, the most unforgettable four hours of night.

My jovial mood returned, and I thanked the Python for not discovering me at night and finding me absolutely uninteresting. Sometimes, I really pity reptiles, which I think I should not, as they have an ancient lineage and have been around for millions of years, surviving various environmental changes. Their resilience and adaptability are remarkable and as pets, reptiles require minimal grooming, they don't shed fur or feathers, and don't require to be taken out for walks, Perfect for busy lifestyles or apartment living. However, our vision has evolved to spot snake shapes and patterns even before conscious awareness, triggering a fearful reaction. But man is the troublemaker who sneaks into every nook and corner and disturbs everyone else's habitats. Look at us. We intrude upon their territory and still blame them for being ferocious! What a pity!

Though I was trying to keep my mood light-hearted, with every passing second, my patience was turning into frustration, but even at this moment, I did not give up hope. I knew that very soon the flying school would discover that one of the aircrafts was missing. They would soon track me through the GPS or the one of the civilian apps available at the airport or the school or with one of my school friends. In this world of advanced technology, they would surely find me. The only catch was that they had to do so before any of the predatory creatures found me, or my degrading wound consumed me. I had to remain alive physically, and sane, both emotionally and mentally. Patience and optimism were my only strengths, it seemed, at that moment.

My mind raced to contemplate what they would do to find me. During our training we were trained on the Emergency Locator Transmitters (ELT) systems in the aircraft which has played a crucial role in rescuing aircrafts and occupants during emergencies, especially during crash sites in remote areas. We were told that the

ELTs are either automatically activated by impact or can be manually activated, which I was not able to do after the crash. When activated, the ELTs transmit a distress signal that can be detected by non-geostationary satellites.

I was not sure if my aircraft's ELT got activated or was it transmitting any signal. When ELTs transmit their GPS position, Search and rescue teams can locate them precisely using GPS trilateration and doppler triangulation. More than twenty aeroplanes must have flown over me, but I didn't see any coming to rescue me. I remembered the flight patterns taught to us that are made by pilots make when they are involved in a Search and Rescue mission–circular patterns, especially if they repeat, may indicate a search, and low and slow flying could be a sign of search efforts as well. But I didn't see any of the planes making these flight patterns. I thought of signaling my presence by flashing anything reflective, but I couldn't find anything other than the glass of the watch which I was wearing, even though the watch had stopped working because it was submerged in the swamp water. I started waving the red cushions which were made to be bright and attractive to enable detection during SAR, however, despite doing that for next 4 hours, I still saw no sign of help. I was starting to feel helpless. I shouted at the top of my lungs many times but failed to catch anyone's attention. I sat down to conserve my energy, for I had no idea how much time it would take for help to arrive, *IF* it was going to arrive.

The chilly night had turned into a bright day and without a piece of cloth on my upper body I could feel the Sun burning me. The same sunlight which I was craving, had now become my enemy. The sudden transition from the cold to blazing heat creates a vivid contrast, making the Sun feel even more powerful.

I grabbed my bag again and looked for my belongings which had survived the landing. I found two packets of oatmeal in the bag. They were wet. I remember taking them out to dry just in case I needed them later. Just as I was doing that, I heard my school's aircraft circling right over me. I immediately stood up and waved the red cushions with all my might. Surprisingly, I could stand up with the broken heel and a badly injured right leg. There was no sensation of pain at that moment, nothing else mattered at that time. That was the moment I had been waiting for since yesterday, ever since the crash. This sight of the aircraft from my school had kept me going. I knew it. I knew they would find me. My joy knew no bounds as I waved the bright red coloured cushions frantically to catch their attention. God forbid, what if they missed seeing me and just went past me without noticing me! Yes, they had seen me. Finally! I was found. Thank God. I had been traced. My ordeal would finally be over now. They would do something to extricate me, I started wondering how. "Be patient," I told myself, just hold on for some more time."

But alas, my state of abandonment wasn't over yet. They came close to me, close enough for me to see the pilot clearly. He was a young, clean-shaven guy along with an accomplice, almost the same age. They came close, and then they left. A deafening cacophony of questions started running through my head–Why on earth were they going back? Had they failed to spot me? Was I hallucinating, like I had the previous night? Was this place a haven of spirits? I failed to come up with an answer for any of these questions.

My heart started to sink. This had to be a mistake, a *faux pax*! I was so sure of it! They could not go back like this. They had seen me. Surely, they would come back when they would not find me anywhere at the school or my homestay. They had traced my location after all. They could not give up so easily. It was terrible to see freedom so near, but not be able to attain it. I sat down on the wing of the aircraft that had been my rustic abode since last night. My mind was racing for some way to attract them. I looked at the sky for a clue. That's when it happened.

I saw a helicopter, then one more, and yet two more. Then it finally hit me–big time, the crash, the chances of death, my survival, everything hit me all at once. In one flash, a fleeting glance at all the events that had occurred since the time I boarded the Cessna. I looked around one last time and was sure that I did not want to visit this place again under similar circumstances. No way. Never. They were finally coming for me.

The plane from the flying school became visible again, followed by the first helicopter which was from the Fire department, the second was the Sheriff of the nearest town. The third helicopter had a doctor and two medics from a local hospital. There was yet another helicopter from a news agency. I was given live coverage, and every moment of the rescue operation was covered. Within moments, my rescue was streaming on almost all news channels across *Florida.*

One of the helicopters had come so close to the crashed plane that I could see the Sheriff inside the helicopter. The first thought that flashed through my mind was, "My God! What a cool guy!" He spoke to me through the microphone as the sound of the hovering helicopter was too high. He asked me if I was okay to which I gestured with a thumbs up. He appreciated my courage and assured me that the situation was under control. Next, he asked me if I was injured, and I raised my thumb up again. I saw him saying something to the other man in the helicopter. He then directed the men inside the third helicopter which was from the local Fire Department.

I could hear my heart pounding with excitement. Just a matter of minutes, I told myself, but that was not the case. It took them almost another half an hour to get into a position that would allow the helicopter to hover, so that someone could come down and get me. A man from the rescue helicopter jumped down with a bungee rope. He landed on the wing of the semi-submerged Cessna which was my abode for past 9 hours. He prepped and hooked me. I picked up my bag and gladly clung on to the rope and found much solace and security in his touch. I had been longing for human touch. I had been yearning for some connection with civilization, in whichever way possible.

The moment I landed on safe ground, the sheriff came running to me with his arms wide open to embrace me. He hugged me like a parent does his long-lost child. I can still feel the strength with which he had hugged me, and the sincerity in his emotion. He shouted at the top of his voice, "Everything is going to be okay. You are the first pilot to have emerged out of *Everglades* alive."

He congratulated me for remaining alive among the deadliest of animals! He kept saying that everything was going to be alright, and I need not worry. The worst battle was over. He kept reassuring me that all the arrangements had been made, and I could see that.

Amidst the deafening sound of the helicopters, I could hear him distinctly. This again brought a wide smile to my face, despite the fatigue. I have no words to describe those moments. These strangers felt like close family to me, they were my saviours. I had made history. Not that I was particularly proud of myself for making headlines in this manner, but I was hugely relieved, humbled, and thankful.

We reached the hospital in about fifteen minutes. The helicopter landed on the roof of one of the buildings. The staff was ready with the stretcher, and I was carried to the dressing room in some other building, through an elevator. Once in the dressing room, a thorough disinfection process was applied on my wounds.

Again, to my surprise, everyone talked to me, but no one asked me any questions which was so strange. Generally, the patient or the victim of an accident is asked many questions about the accident to know what kind of treatment needs to be given, but no one asked me anything. At the same time, they seemed to know exactly what needed to be done. Later, I was enlightened that the story of the *Everglades* was not new to anyone at the hospital. They knew exactly what needed to be done. The area was notorious for being insect infested.

I was told that the wounds were full of infection from the dirty water of the lake but there was nothing to worry about. I wanted to tell them that this issue seemed petty in comparison to what I had gone through the previous night. Nothing ever could be compared to the mental trauma of being there all alone for a good nine hours, but I was thankful that the injuries were not fatal, nonetheless.

Next came the doctor and two medics with their boxes and other paraphernalia. The doctor welcomed me with a big smile and assured me that I looked great. He examined my wound first. The first external human touch was painful, very painful. It was the first cognizance of excruciating pain. For the first time I was reminded of the ghastly wound and how I had not paid any attention to it. The medics cleaned the wound thoroughly with saline water and temporarily fixed the hanging calf muscles in the best possible manner. They examined my nose, eyes, pulse and other body vitals. Once assured that my medical condition was under control, I was made to sit in the helicopter that had carried the doctor and was admitted to the local hospital.

Very soon, I was shifted to the operation theatre where the surgeon, Dr Kelly, smiled at me kindly. She was also full of admiration for me for surviving the most dangerous habitat in *Florida*. She was a retired army officer, yet another connection with my life. The assistant doctor made small talk with me and asked me to 'sniff the stuff'.

I was given anaesthesia and after that I had no idea what they did to me. I had drifted to the Land of Nod. In my subconscious mind, I commended myself for being hopeful by maintaining a calm and serene demeanour.

Yet another miracle had happened. Another operation, where one moment I was to meet my death, and the other moment I lived. The only difference was that this time the combat time was nine long hours instead of a moment of realization that my mother had! The first miracle on the operation table embarked me on a journey of nine months before my entry into the world, and this rescue 'operation' lasted nine hours. I am forced to believe now that though man has a free will, he is destined to meet his fate. Everything that happens to you during your lifetime, happens for a reason. Nothing happens just like that.

Surprisingly, the whole rescue operation had taken almost two hours after I was spotted by the team sent by the flying school. I still wondered why it had taken so long for them to spot me. The mystery did not unfold itself until I reached the hospital and met my housemates after the surgery.

I was told later that the first person to identify my absence was my housemate, *Diya*, who shared our car with me. When she woke up that morning to get ready for her flight which was scheduled for eight o'clock, she found the car missing. She looked around everywhere but could not spot me. She spoke to other housemates and investigated the matter thinking someone else might have taken the car or I would have gone with someone else. She soon found out that I had not returned from the flight at all.

It was seven in the morning at that time. This raised an alarm. She immediately reported it to the school authorities. But since the owner arrived at the school only at ten, her pleas did not yield much of a result. She reached the school and called up the owner to explain the seriousness of the situation, which made the whole process further delayed. The owner acted from home as soon as she got to know about my absence. I had texted all the details of the flight and the aircraft to her the night before, as was the norm before any flight. She contacted the Fire Rescue Department and the Sheriff personally. The officials were questioning her which led to a lot of time being wasted. She lost her cool and threatened to send her own team from the school to look for me, which she eventually did.

Diya had traced the location of my aircraft through one of the civilian apps, which was the point where my Cessna had gone spiraling down. This further added to the delay in identifying my exact location.

I gave myself a big pat on the back for being able to get reborn in the very womb of Mother Nature. I was thankful to God for being so kind and for supporting me with my planning. The strategy that I had conceived and executed was possible only because the time was favourable. My guardian angels were there all the time to keep me patient and hopeful. They were guiding me to do the right thing at the right moment. The symphony of sounds that would have scared any ordinary person was music to my ears and the eerie specters that could have given any ordinary man a heart attack gave me resilience to endure the trauma. My calmness and presence of mind was my strength.

Inside the operation theatre, my conscious mind was not aware of my surroundings, but my subconscious mind was active. It relived the entire trauma, and the stark reality of the situation struck me only after the surgery. Inside the ward, when I recovered from the effects of anaesthesia, I realized that it was my second birth indeed, but the struggle was not over yet. A long and more painful journey lay ahead.

This would require every ounce of my will power, patience, and perseverance to overcome the challenges of the aftermath. I would require the support of my friends. In the absence of the family, I craved to be with my friends–all of them.

A calm mind, which acts as a linchpin for mental strength, not only shields individuals from the corrosive effects of stress but also empowers them to face life's challenges with resilience and grace. My calmness during hard times was going to come to my rescue in the forthcoming battle. I earnestly prayed that I would recover from my physical injuries and resume flying but somehow, I knew intuitively that it was not going to be easy, and definitely not in the immediate future. But I told myself that I would worry about it later.

My ebbing strength was not letting my subconscious mind act anymore, and I eventually gave up. I needed to take rest and rejuvenate completely before embarking upon my next journey. Whether it is a cancer survivor finding hope during treatment or a person rebuilding their life after a devastating loss, the emotional fortitude derived from hope is a testament to its transformative power. It is the emotional light that pierces through the darkness, enabling individuals to persevere and emerge stronger on the other side. The emotional resilience of hope was evident in me even in that state of slumber, and I was preparing myself for the forthcoming challenges.

"The fact that you woke up this morning is proof that this day has already been predetermined in your favour."

CHAPTER 8
THE ROAD TO RECOVERY

योगस्थः कुरु कर्माणि सङ्गं त्यक्त्वा धनञ्जय।
सिद्ध्यसिद्ध्योः समो भूत्वा समत्वं योग उच्यते।।[25]

(In this, Lord Krishna advises Arjuna to perform his duties with an evenness of mind, without getting attached to the outcome. He emphasizes the importance of detachment and encourages Arjuna to focus on the present moment and the task at hand, rather than worrying about the future or regretting the past.)

Patience is not just the ability to wait. It is how you behave while waiting for the right time and the right things to happen. I had read a lot about stoicism when I was in school. I am particularly fascinated by the writings of Marcus Aurelius and his philosophy of stoicism. He insists on the fact that at the time of adversity, one is more frightened of one's judgement about the situation, rather than the actual situation itself. I think I was also doing the same and this knowledge about stoic behaviour helped me pull myself out from moments of self-doubt.

Doubts like "Will I be able to walk properly again?", "Will I be able to fly again?", "What would be the result of the enquiry?" or "Would I would get a clean chit or not?", kept bothering me for many weeks and took my frustration to another level. Had I not been aware of the concept of stoic behaviour, I would not have been able to phase out of this mental condition after the surgery. There were two back-to-back surgeries, and the recovery was to at a slow speed. So, the aftermath of the accident was more formidable than the accident itself.

I have no idea how long I was in the operation theatre for. When I finally woke up from my deep sleep, I was in the waiting room where several other patients, who were still recovering from the effect of the anaesthesia, were lying in their beds.

On seeing me tossing over in the bed, the nurses came to check my body vitals and made some small talk to ensure that all was well and there were no major aftereffects of the sedation. I was told that it would take another twenty minutes to take me to the room.

The first person who I saw in the waiting room was the owner of the flying school. Her worried face turned to a one with a faint smile after seeing me on the hospital bed. She said she had never felt so relieved than when I recognized her and smiled faintly at her. She congratulated me for being alive and enduring the trauma so stoically, that history was created. She said that I would be an unforgettable student for her, and she would remember me with a peculiar fondness and affection that she had never felt before for anyone. She told me not to worry a bit about the aircraft and asked me earnestly what she could do for me.

She informed me that *Diya*, *Christian* and *Bhumika* from the flying school were waiting outside to see me but were being denied entry primarily to avoid any media attention and, secondly, visitors would only be allowed to meet me in the room. She had been given special permission as she had taken the responsibility in the absence of my family. She asked me if I was hungry, and I moved my head in affirmation. She got me orange juice and 'chicken panini'. I relished the orange juice as it was the first sip of liquid I had taken after the crash. It tasted heavenly as it quenched my thirst and soothed my parched throat. I remembered I had asked for water before being taken into the OT but since I had to be operated upon, I was refused. The first morsel of the 'chicken panini' was also divine. I could hear churning sounds coming from my stomach and I relished every bite of the 'delicacy'. I had eaten nothing for the past twenty-four hours.

When I was shifted to the room, she gave me a pen and paper to write about the accident. I wrote just four or five lines and gave up due to lack of strength. And when my house mates finally arrived to see me, she left but only after being reassured that *Diya and Christian* would stay with me for the night. Her concern looked genuine, and it touched me. *Diya*, *Christian* and *Bhumika* had no clue about my injury, the surgery, and my current state. They evidently looked worried and scared. They felt better and looked relieved after speaking to me. They took care of every need of mine.

The owner of the flying school told me that my parents had been informed and they wished to talk to me. She also told me that *Major DP Singh* had called for me. On being asked who I wanted to talk to first, without a second thought, I requested her to connect me to Major DP Singh first. He was in India at the time. She made me talk to him on video call immediately. The moment he took the call and I saw his face on the screen, I broke down. I felt as if I was with a family member who was very close to me. I cried for the first time since the accident. I had been enduring all the struggle, pain, and grief stoically, all alone, until then, keeping a brave front. I cried bitterly for a good five minutes. He did not stop me. He neither interrupted me nor did he try to say anything to console me. Not a single word came from him. Gradually my loud wailing turned into hysterical sobbing and finally subsided with silent moaning. He just let me cry. I felt extremely relieved as if a big burden had been off my chest. Such was his presence for me!

Two questions occurred to me later. I wondered what made me want to talk to him even before my Dad or Mom. And, secondly, what made me cry like a child on seeing him on the screen of the phone. I had never been very close to him, after all. I had known about him and found him truly inspiring at the flying school. Major DP Singh has been a source of inspiration to many. Besides joking around with him on several occasions I had not really spent so much time with him at the flying school, but strangely, I felt close to him then. He mesmerizes everyone around him with his zeal for life. Such was his demeanour; you couldn't help being impressed by him. I concluded that it was the expression of affection in his eyes that triggered my emotional outburst. The expression in his eyes was so intense, honest, and sincere that all my pent-up feelings came rolling down my cheeks in a stream of tears. He finally smiled at me and said that he was glad to see me alive. He addressed me as "*Mera Sher Bachcha*" ('My lion cub' implying that I was just as courageous.) That did the magic.

He assured me that everything would soon be back to normal, and I believed him, that very instant, without further questions. There was no doubt now that anything could go wrong. He assured me that the streak of courage was an inherited trait in me, and I had lived up to it making everyone proud of me. Before I proceed, let me tell you very briefly about him. This will justify my decision to talk to him though at that time it was made intuitively, at the spur of the moment.

Major DP Singh, a retired officer of the Indian Army, is a Kargil War veteran and is known as India's first Blade Runner. After his amputation, he gradually started running using a prosthetic limb and has run in 26 half-marathons in his running career. This includes three half-marathons in extreme altitude as high as 11,700 ft (3,600 m) in Leh. The Limca Book of Records added his name to their "People of the Year" list in 2016. In 2018, Government of India, Ministry of Social Justice and Empowerment conferred him with National award for persons with disabilities under Role Model category. In 2019 he was conferred with the coveted civilian award, CavinKare Ability Mastery award in recognition of excellence achieved against all odds. He was taken as the Ambassador by Indian Army for the year 2018, which was the year dedicated to soldiers who got disabled in the line of duty. In 2019, he wrote another chapter in history when he became the first solo Skydiver among persons with disabilities in all of Asia. You see why he inspires all those who meet or read about him? He has aachieved so much in life despite the disabilities he had due to the war. His life story was chronicled in *Grit: The Major Story*, a 2019 graphic memoir that he co-authored with *V.R. Ferose* and *Sriram Jagannathan.*

When I broke down in front of him, he told me that we should be grateful for what we still have and not lament for what we have lost. Losses are bound to happen. Every human being must endure pain in one's lifetime. Losses are inevitable, irrevocable, and inescapable. So, the best was to accept them and overcome them as soon as possible. I requested him to consult the doctor and tell me the true status of my injuries. He knew the fear was gnawing at me from the inside. He said whatever it was, it should not bother me, and I should only think about recovering soon.

The team of doctors who had operated upon me arrived in the room soon after and told me that they had managed to remove the infection from the calf muscles and sewed the entire piece of mass together. According to them, the calf muscles would take less time to heal than the other areas. They had also operated upon the heel but there was a hairline fracture, and the recovery would be comparatively slow. The surgery was not an easy one as the dangling heel had to be put in the proper place without further damaging the fractured area.

On the second day, *Diya and Christian* went back home and Umair, my friend from Jammu, stayed with me. The room was quite uninteresting. It had a T.V. but nothing interesting was playing on any of the channels so we talked about everything under the Sun. There was a vacuum cleaner advertisement which played all night long, so weird that we made silly jokes about it. The next morning. Tired from sleeping on hospital sofa, an exhausted and worn out *Umair* went downstairs to get some coffee for himself, and I requested to take a few sips which he gladly shared with me and let me have it all, so were my friends. He asked me who I wanted to come next. I told him to let *Raghav* come. *Raghav* wanted to come but unfortunately, he couldn't make it. Despite being only a forty-five-minute flight away, the weather took a turn for the worse, forcing him to abort the flight.

On that very day, three people from Federal Aviation Administration (FAA), had come for a routine enquiry about the crash. *Raghav* had already cautioned me about the inquiry and advised me to be honest with them. They were so experienced that they could make out in a jiffy if someone was lying. Besides, he assured me that their motive was not to ruin any pilot's career. Their only purpose was to figure out the real reason for the crash. So, I was mentally prepared to face them. One of the officers seemed to be in a hurry as he hurled question after question at me. He blatantly asked me if I vaped or was into drugs? If I had consumed alcohol before the flight? There were also some routine questions asked from me. The second team member was a woman who kept quiet and observed me closely as if trying to gauge my mental state. She did not utter a single word throughout the meeting. The third was a middle-aged man with salt-and-pepper hair. He made me feel comfortable by just indulging in small talk. His name was *Antonio*. He was the only one among all three who showed sympathy and even offered to help in future if I needed any.

On the third day, the doctors told me to try and walk with the help of the crutches. The attempt was frightening. My right leg had two injuries. The calf muscles had been sown back and the heel had a hairline fracture. There was no movement in that leg. I was told not to put the entire body weight on the left leg and balance it out with the help of the crutches. I was supposed to maintain balance by putting the tip of my left foot on the floor. The moment I kept my left foot down on the ground, I felt excruciating pain as there was no blood circulation due to zero movement after the surgery.

For a few moments, I was aghast with the thought that movement would not be possible at all. My heart must have skipped a few beats, I am sure of that. But soon enough the nurse and ward boys came to me with encouraging words like, "honey, you can do it." Another said, "Honey, it is normal, try once again." Yet another pleasant voice said, "Honey, keep the left leg gently once again. It is simple." Sooner than I thought, I was able to take a small round inside the room with their help. This was quite encouraging. I marvelled at how supportive and motivating the entire staff was.

Dr Kelly; the tall, beautiful, blue-eyed, blonde doctor; had been a thorough professional right from the beginning who commanded respect from me. From the moment I entered the hospital on a stretcher from the helipad to the trauma room, she had been caring and affectionate but in a very detached manner. Paradoxical, it may sound, but it was true. Her soft yet commanding voice was music to my ears every time she spoke to me. She would command the nurses and the paramedics to be gentle with me and hold my leg in a particular way to avoid any pain or inconvenience to me. She was an awe-inspiring woman. I had made a special mention of this later when I went to get my stitches removed from her. She smiled at me and didn't say a word. Her smile said it all. I would sing songs in her praise to all the housemates in the hospital and they would tease me for that. But my admiration for her was honestly for her professional excellence.

I remember, back at the house, some days later, somebody had asked me how many days I had spent at the hospital. I told him that it was exactly four days and three nights. It sounded like a vacation package to me. I was glad that this second chapter of trauma that had just begun had not killed my humour. I was still getting weird and funny thoughts proving the fact that I was doing well but it was not going to last long. I had to struggle hard to keep my cheerfulness and wittiness alive.

After being discharged from the hospital, I was taken to the homestay where all the housemates were extraordinarily caring. They cared for every minute detail that was a challenge for me after the accident. It was all very new for all of us. I was trying to cope with the feeling of restriction, and they were struggling to keep my movement hassle free. They all were young and inexperienced, and along with that they had their busy schedules. I was free the whole day with nothing to do but crib over the limited movement, pain in the wounds, feelings of dependency, helplessness, and frustration.

A free spirit who had never faced any kind of restriction at home or here, a pilot who was used to flying at his own free will was now lying like a crippled man watching others moving ahead gaily in their lives. Their being healthy was not what bothered me, but my own limitations were becoming unbearable day by day. This sentiment was becoming more powerful with the passing of days. The simple gestures by them for making my life easy and painless also started becoming a cause of my anger. Anger started building up so much that I started screaming over little things. My irritability kept increasing and the outbursts of anger became more frequent.

The first time I threw a tantrum stupefied everyone. One day, while two friends were helping me get into my wheelchair, they fussed over me and cautioned me to be still, or I may hurt myself. I just do not know what came over me at that moment, and I lost it completely. I screamed at them at the top of my voice and told them that they were creating a scene and were being dramatic unnecessarily. I told them that there was no need to pity me, and I could not take their condescending behaviour anymore. I was told later by other friends who happened to witness the whole affair that I was quite harsh. There was stunned silence for about a couple of minutes after I stopped being exhausted both physically and emotionally. The two friends just patted me on my back and left without a word.

Later when my anger subsided, I apologized to both several times out of shame and guilt and they were humble enough to tell me that I should not even think about it again. They only tried to reassure me that they were genuinely trying to help me and had no intention of looking down upon me. And, of course, I knew that. But it was not easy for me to remain calm anymore.

This incident had happened a week after my discharge from the hospital. The owner of the flying school visited the house the very next day. She must have heard about it from my friends. It was a pleasant surprise though. She was usually very strict with all the students at the school, but that day, we were all in for a surprise. My housemates were busy in the late evening with chores like cooking preparations when the doorbell rang. Everyone was amazed to see her entering with bags loaded with dinner. She seemed to be in a happy mood. She announced that all of us should stop cooking and assemble at the dining table for a nice chat together over dinner as she had ordered food for all of us. She said she felt like celebrating my coming home.

We all had a great time together and were a little puzzled to see this other side of her. After winding up for dinner, out of respect, everyone excused themselves and left both of us to talk in private. She discussed the incident of the previous day and shared the difficulties she had to face when she had moved to the US at a very young age from India. She told me that she started with just three dollars and seventy cents and a whole lot of hope. She had to struggle for years before she finally started reaping the profits of her hard work.

There had been more situations of failures than successes and she had learnt hugely from the mistakes she had made in the initial years of starting the flying school. She told me that everyone must overcome hardships with patience and perseverance and and its not over for me yet. She advised me to remain positive and not get frustrated. She advised me to read motivational books and listen to podcasts by motivational speakers. I was thankful to her for being concerned and affectionate. I also expressed my gratitude that she had taken out time to counsel me like this.

The next day, *Umair* took me to my favourite spot near the lake . There was a lake inside the society where our house was. I used to spend a lot of time there alone. That day, he took me there in a wheelchair and counselled me about my inappropriate behaviour the day before. He was disturbed at the fact that my mental health needed immediate attention.

He advised me to maintain a journal to keep my anger under control as it would be disastrous for me in the end. Any negative emotion when it becomes uncontrollable, consumes one's relationships, he said. He explained to me that everyone in the house was genuinely trying to help me and if I continued to behave like that, they would soon stop being understanding. This would surely end the friendships I had developed with all of them. This made a lot of sense to me. I knew in the core of my heart that I had not behaved appropriately but the truth of the matter was that it was the result of my own frustration and helplessness and nothing else. It was certainly not intended at them but at myself. At the same time, there was no excuse for it.

One constant thought that I had was the quote " a good captain goes down with the ship" in my mind my ship went down but I survived, I later had to relearn the phrase and change my perspective about the whole quote.

What made me behave like that? During the time I spent in the hospital and later at home when I was unable to walk around and felt almost crippled and frustrated at, I started reading more books on stoicism, coping strategies and how to look forward to a hopeful future despite the injury which was taking longer to heal than I had expected. The doubtfulness of complete recovery that bothered me so much in the beginning had to be tackled. Dealing with my frustration about my recovery required more *stoicism* than the actual accident itself. The time post the surgery was something that required a hundred times more patience, perseverance, and resilience. For how long could I keep wishing for a speedy recovery when the facts were contrary to my expectations?

I remember another incident when we were at the dinner table, and I was in the wheelchair. I was talking to my folks in India. There was something about the car that I got to know only at that moment when all others knew about it. Though it was a petty issue, I lost my temper and broke my crutches accusing everyone of hiding things from me just because they thought I was crippled now. They did not find it necessary to share both mundane and important things with me. I knew the accusation was baseless, but I continued with my rant for quite some time. No one retaliated and allowed me to vent out my anger.

Now, when I look back and think about it, I feel so childish. How could I behave so naively? I clearly remember that before the owner of the flying school or *Umair* had counselled me about the anger management, my Dad had cautioned me about it. He said that I would begin to imagine that people around me were pitying me, and their genuine concerns or innocent remarks would sound like taunts. He had told me about this phase much before it happened to me. Everyone in my family and my housemates seemed to be ready for this. They were patient, caring and accommodating. No one would react when I misbehaved in a fit of anger but empathized with me. They understood that it was not my true self but just a passing phase. A young boy who was flying for more than four to five hours a day, was now confined to his bed. This was indeed nothing less than mental and physical torture.

I had read somewhere a long time back that life is divided into three periods, past, present, and future. Of these, the present is short, the future is doubtful, the past is certain. With the certainty that the present injuries were going to take more time to heal than expected, there was no point in wasting time worrying about the future. This also did not mean that I gave up hope and stopped dreaming. I knew I shall recover and positively pursue my dream of soaring high in the sky amidst the clouds, but this time with humility and gratitude. So, the present required me to work on honing my mental skills by pursuing other interests such as reading, which could not be carried forward earlier because of the adventurous endeavours I had always preferred to indulge in.

Patience and mindfulness were now my keys to happiness in the present circumstances. I had earlier decided to remain in the US as I was sure that I would recover soon and resume flying. I could not have returned without completing the course. Even when the response from the doctors and my body were rather bleak, I knew deep inside my heart that I would achieve my goal in life, no matter what. But now, the situation was not entirely in my hands. I tried to walk around with crutches despite the pain, but it was not doing any good. I was not recovering, I knew it. I, finally, decided to fly to India and be with my family till I began walking.

"Fortitude means fixity of purpose. It means endurance. It means having the strength to live with what constrains you."

PAINT SHO
adidas

CHAPTER 9
FORGING AHEAD WITH FORTITUDE

तेजः क्षमा धृतिः शौचमद्रोहो नातिमानिता।
भवन्ति सम्पदं दैवीमभिजातस्य भारत॥[26]

(Vigour, forgiveness, fortitude, purity, absence of hatred, absence of pride — these belong to the one born for the Divine Estate, O Bharata.)

Fortitude is like an unwavering flame within us, allowing us to persist even when circumstances seem unfavourable. It encourages us to stay resolute in our pursuits, regardless of challenges or setbacks. Just as a mountain stands firm against storms, our inner strength enables us to move forward with courage and determination.

"To achieve freedom and happiness, you need to grasp this basic truth: some things in life are under your control, and others are not." — *Epictetus*, a former slave who rose to become one of the greatest Stoic thinkers.

My fascination with stoicism grew stronger when I returned to India in the third week of November. I had a lot of time on my hands to pursue my love for reading. I found reading therapeutic as it helped me heal and recover post the surgery. The books that I read during this time were '*Meditations*' by *Marcus Aurelius* and '*Man in Search of Meaning*' by *Viktor Frankl*. These two books have transformed me as a person, not that I was a spoiled brat earlier or was not able to handle life, but the accident, the aftermath, and the knowledge I got from these books has made me wiser. I now value nature, the facilities that I have by virtue of my birth, my family, friends, and all the medics, para medics, ward boys, nurses, the rescue team members, the Sheriff, all the people who influenced my life in some way or the other, more than I would have done, if this accident would not have happened.

I often wonder, even now, from where I got the strength to endure the aftermath of the accident which was more nightmarish than the accident itself? *Viktor Frankl's* experiences gave me hope and a sense of calmness and tranquility. It inspired me to reflect on the deeper purpose of my life and to find strength in the face of challenges. It is a poignant exploration of the human condition amidst the horrors of the Holocaust. Through his harrowing experiences in Nazi concentration camps, *Frankl* delves into the depths of human suffering and resilience, offering profound insights into the importance of finding meaning in life, even in the most desperate circumstances. One of the central messages of the book is that while individuals cannot always control their external circumstances, they can choose their response to those circumstances. *Frankl* emphasizes the power of attitude and inner strength, suggesting that even in the face of unimaginable suffering, individuals can find meaning and purpose by focusing on their values, relationships, and inner spiritual resources. He argues that those who have a clear sense of purpose and meaning are better equipped to endure suffering and find hope amidst despair. Through his own experiences and those of his fellow prisoners, *Frankl* illustrates the transformative power of finding meaning amid adversity, offering a powerful testament to the resilience of the human spirit. This book resonated with my present circumstances and emotions.

The other book which has become my Bible for living life is '*Meditations*' by *Marcus Aurelius*. It is a timeless treasure trove of wisdom that offers profound lessons on life, virtue, and resilience. Through his personal reflections and philosophical musings, Aurelius imparts invaluable insights that continue to appeal to readers across generations. One of the key takeaways for me from this book is the importance of embracing the present moment and accepting things as they are. *Aurelius* encourages readers to cultivate mindfulness and equanimity, recognizing that the only moment we truly have control over is the present. By letting go of attachment to the past and worries about the future, individuals can find inner peace and contentment in the present circumstances.

Another crucial lesson is the practice of virtue and moral integrity in all aspects of life. *Aurelius* emphasizes the importance of acting with kindness, compassion, and integrity, regardless of external circumstances or temptations. He underscores the notion that true happiness and fulfillment come from living in accordance with one's principles and values. Furthermore, this book teaches one the importance of embracing adversity as an opportunity for growth and self-improvement. This is a lesson that I will remember throughout my life and probably another reason why I decided to make this accident and struggle a memorable affair. *Aurelius* reminds readers that challenges and hardships are inevitable aspects of life, but it is our response to them that defines our character. By cultivating resilience, perseverance, and inner strength, individuals can transform obstacles into opportunities for personal development and spiritual evolution. The reading served as a profound guidebook for me to comprehend the complexities of existence with wisdom, grace, and philosophical insight, inspiring me to live with purpose, integrity, and inner peace.

I learnt that self-knowledge serves as a guiding light on the journey towards inner peace and happiness, illuminating the pathways of understanding, acceptance, and growth. Through introspection and reflection, individuals gain insight into their deepest desires, fears, strengths, and limitations, fostering a profound sense of self-awareness. With this awareness comes the capacity to recognize and acknowledge one's emotions, thoughts, and behaviors with clarity and compassion.

As individuals cultivate a deeper understanding of themselves, they develop a sense of authenticity and alignment with their true selves, enabling them to live in harmony with their values and aspirations. While struggling to control my outbursts, I tried to recognize my true self–a peace-loving person who makes friends with ease and has a way with animals. I genuinely love humanity, I love life. Now I need to learn to respect it.

Self-knowledge empowers individuals to face life's challenges with resilience and grace, as they possess a solid foundation of inner strength and conviction. By embracing their unique identities and embracing their flaws as integral parts of their humanity, individuals cultivate a sense of wholeness and acceptance, freeing themselves from the burden of self-judgement and comparison.

In this state of inner peace and acceptance, individuals experience a profound sense of fulfillment and contentment, grounded in the realization that true happiness emanates from within and is not dependent on external circumstances. Thus, one thing became clear to me, that to live a life well-lived, fostering a deep sense of peacefulness and happiness was essential, and people around me could help me achieve this to a certain extent but primarily, I had to strive for it myself.

The lessons of wisdom given by Dad, Major DP Singh, Carlos, other friends or the counsellor and lessons learnt from the books I was reading, all started making sense and I began to make a conscious effort to internalize all the learning.

When I came to India, I was still in a wheelchair, and movement with crutches was restricted. I tried my best to move around but the pain was not subsiding a bit. This was alarming and my Dad felt that a second opinion was mandatory. On the second day itself, I was taken to the hospital for a second opinion. The doctor saw my wound and almost instantly was convinced that the condition was not good and needed immediate attention.

The doctors investigated the matter and concluded that there was yet more infection in the heel area and a second surgery was recommended. If we delayed the surgery and the infection affected the bone, it could lead to irreversible damage to the leg and could cripple me for a lifetime. This led to an immediate nod from all of us. Some tests were done to check the nature of bacterial infection to decide upon the treatment and medication.

The results of the tests took around three days to arrive, and the surgery was conducted thereafter. The operation concluded successfully but it was a challenging one, as the skin from the ankle was stretched far more than in any ordinary situation. A metal plate was also inserted in front of the leg. The healing was very slow and complete bed rest was advised. I was told that movement and constant suspension of the infected leg right after the first surgery done in the US resulted in the opening of the stitches as well as the wounds. So, a complete bed rest for at least two months was mandatory.

I was also warned to keep the operated leg always elevated. I was given antibiotics through a drip for quick recovery for almost two weeks which was inconvenient and exasperating. The intravenous antibacterial therapy was required as the nature of infection was severe. I was bound to the bed with nothing to do at all, whereas all my other friends were enjoying their lives as I used to before. Watching their posts and reels on social media was becoming unbearable for me. This rocketed my anger and frustration to another level, and I started screaming at everyone around me even more. I missed the hectic routine I had at the flying school. The flying slots, preparation for written exams, moving around with friends–I missed everything so terribly. This was the time when I started therapeutic treatment on my own, but of course, with the aid of my family members. I knew that I had to make a conscious effort to come out of this unhealthy mental condition.

I started maintaining a journal more regularly which I had begun writing in the US. In the beginning, I would write cuss words in the journal whenever I lost my temper with anyone or when a particular situation was beyond my control, and I had a strong urge to scream all these cuss words at the top of my voice.

Later, I started writing about the things that appealed to me or disturbed me. Very soon, I graduated to recording my feelings and writing about all the things I wished to do the moment I was ready to move around followed by all those things which I would do upon my complete recovery. I even visualized my return to the US to continue the course from where I had left it. I planned to speed up of the process of Time Building that had been discontinued because of the accident. I wrote down every minute detail. This gave me enough clarity about the future and calmed me down to a great extent. It was a beautiful and interesting distraction.

On a lighter note, writing so much in the journal daily was a strenuous job in the beginning. I marveled at my ability to write so much. I gradually started enjoying it. I would look forward to this time during the day. This kept me happily distracted as I would keep thinking about new ideas to pen down. I discovered for the first time in life that creative writing could also be addictive. But this was not enough to pass the time, so I thought of indulging in other activities which would keep me engaged in a systematic manner. So, I enrolled myself in online courses which I had been wanting to do for quite some time. I successfully completed a course in Geopolitics followed by another course in Russian Literature. Finally, introspection of multiple plans and, at the same time, retrospection about the events that had already happened, helped me calm down.

A realization that is very soothing is that I was in a foreign country among strangers, far away from my real family, but I was indeed blessed to have been surrounded by people who loved me, cared for me, stood by me till the time I flew back to India and even here, my friends are with me all the time. All the friends in the house in *Florida* and the flying school made a valuable contribution in helping me recover. They all were students who had numerous constraints like money, time, and busy schedules, and yet they came forward to help me so lovingly and willingly. Will I ever be able to do this for someone in need? No, I don’t think so, and this fills me with immense gratitude for all of them.

I feel humbled at the thought that I was showered with so much love by everyone around me. Not a single soul around me has shown me either apathy or rudeness so far. I was anxious in the beginning that I would become a target of jibes and people would make fun of me and say that despite becoming a 'hero', I had now failed to succeed in my endeavors but, by God's grace, no one has ever made fun of me or my fate. Whoever has heard of the accident and the harrowing experience has shown me grace and love alone, and I thank God for this. Some divine power seems to be blessing me with heavenly love.

Back in *Bengaluru*, I survived because of my friends. My friend from school, Arjun, visited me frequently and entertained me with his company. He happened to be in the city for his internship. He would even take my calls late at night and would talk to me for hours. What would have I done without my friends? One day, I remember, I called him and told him that I was feeling a bit low that night. He told me to disconnect the phone and he would talk to me in a while. He kept the phone hastily. I found it a little strange but thought that something urgent must have crept up and waited for his call.

There was no call and I forgot all about it. About half an hour later, which was almost midnight, I saw him outside my house. He travelled from another corner of the city to meet me just because I had said that I was feeling a bit low. I hugged him for love. Such are my friends! I am indebted to them all.

I thank God every single day that I'm fortunate enough to have made good and sincere friends whether it was at school, my society, or the flying school. One day all my school friends came to spend the day with me, which was a pleasant surprise for me. We had great fun together till late at night. My friends have been my saving grace. This gives me a reason to come back to the fact that life takes you where you ought to be.

Just a week before New Year's Eve, the stitches were removed, and I could limp around. The day they were removed, I tried to walk. My joy knew no bounds and I made video calls to almost all my close friends in India and in the US to give them the good news. They reciprocated my excitement with the same intensity. Some of them even cried. I was on top of the world. This was such a morale booster. My confidence was back with the hope of a speedy recovery. The first week saw quick progress, which eventually slowed down. During the next couple of weeks, there was no further change. I consulted the doctor for physiotherapy. The doctor told us that it was not required, and I should let things happen slowly, taking their own natural course. But I could not wait for so long and went for physiotherapy sessions anyway. Soon enough, I started walking with the help of a golf stick and then even without it. I am indeed thankful that I have recovered completely from the injury.

The physical injury has healed but some traces of the mental trauma are still visible in my behaviour. I still cannot endure the dim light of the table lamp at night and for that matter, any kind of dim yellow light gives me a sinking feeling. It reminds me of the eerie night I had spent in pale moonlight, and I relive the whole nightmare all over again. I had sought professional help for mental strength back in the US. *Raghav* had recommended an app called Better Help. I had taken around four to five sessions which really helped in the beginning. Once I found my emotions under control, I told myself that I would tackle my feelings on my own. Since childhood, I have handled my emotions on my own, without even seeking help from my parents. I can do it even now. Again, some conscious effort and I will be able to overcome it. I will soon find a way to beat this fear of the pale-yellow light as well.

I have started dreaming again, just like the old times. While awaiting the result of the enquiry, which will not happen before six months from the time of the accident, I have not wasted my time. I have prepared to clear another flying exam called Radio Telephony Restricted. This exam is the toughest one that a trainee pilot should go through to get a commercial pilot licence in India. I had anyway decided to take it after the completion of the course in *Florida*, but now I am doing earlier than planned since I have nothing else to do. Even though it did not work the way I had planned it initially, I am glad that at least life has given me a second chance to do it. How does it matter when it is done? What matters is that I can do it.

So, *Florida*, I am coming back very soon. There are still some airports left where I have not flown to yet with *Diya*, for a sumptuous breakfast. I used to fly with her to different airports for breakfast on Sundays. I miss those fun-filled flights. I am sure it will happen very soon.

Surviving a near-fatal accident has evoked a profound sense of gratitude that now permeates every aspect of my life. In the wake of such a harrowing experience, one's perspective shifts, and the simple joys and blessings of existence become vividly apparent. Every breath becomes a gift, every moment a precious opportunity. Gratitude fills the heart for the chance to continue living, for the second chance granted amidst the uncertainty of mortality. It is a gratitude not just for being alive, but for the resilience of the human spirit, the kindness of strangers, and the love of family and friends that provided support and solace during the darkest hours. This newfound appreciation serves as a guiding light, illuminating the path forward with a profound sense of humility, resilience, and a deeper appreciation for the beauty of life's fleeting moments.

“Gratitude is the single most important ingredient to living a successful and fulfilled life.”

CHAPTER 10
GRATITUDE

तमेव शरणं गच्छ सर्वभावेन भारत|
तत्प्रसादात्परां शान्तिं स्थानं प्राप्स्यसि शाश्वतम् ||[27]

(Surrender exclusively unto Him with your whole being, O Bharat. By His grace, you will attain perfect peace and the eternal abode.)

This verse reminds us to maintain an attitude of gratitude towards God. Reflect on the countless gifts we receive daily—the earth we walk upon, the sunlight that illuminates our days, the air we breathe and the water that sustains us—all bestowed upon us by the Divine. Surrendering wholeheartedly to God leads us to supreme peace and the eternal abode. Gratitude turns what we have into enough and more. It turns denial into acceptance, chaos into order, confusion into clarity...it makes sense of our past, brings peace for today, and creates a vision for tomorrow.

***

I have reached the same point where I started from—*Man plans. God laughs*. In simple words, we human beings can't control our circumstances. The only thing that one person can control is one's actions, reactions, and responses to tackle a particular situation. Even the bleakest hour of one's life can be bettered by learning and practising certain virtues. Based on my personal experience, I can say that if we respond with courage, temperance, wisdom, and justice we can succeed in the direst of conditions also.

I was a carefree student at a flying school in *Florida* who thought himself to be the best in his batch and was forging ahead brimming with confidence and leaving no stone unturned to pursue his passion. The unexpected crash in the *Everglades*, my survival, and the struggle after it, has not killed my spirit and zeal to live life even a small bit. On the contrary, now in addition to the will and passion, I have the conviction that I will be an excellent pilot. I have all the required skills and an indomitable morale and instinct to survive.

I have understood the pettiness as well as the magnanimity of human life. Nine unending hours amidst the most grotesque side of nature showed me the triviality of human life where danger lurked from all sides. I was at the mercy of nature and my destiny. Paradoxically, the same gory side of nature showed me the preciousness of human life. Every minute that I spent there made me value my life. Every breath that I was taking became precious. I loved myself before but superficially, in a gross manner. Now, I love myself more and in a profound manner.

I have also learnt to respect other living beings and recognize the value of life and God's creations. I have understood that our existence in the universe is impossible in isolation. We cannot alienate ourselves from other creatures on this earth and a mutual coexistence is necessary.

I have understood what it means to have a strong character. A person who has embodied moral values and practises them as a way of life, can never remain unsuccessful for long.

As children we are made to pray to be thankful for all that God has given us. We all do it mindlessly for years. But now I thank God mindfully. I am grateful that I am alive today. The fact that no pilot has ever survived a crash in the *Everglades* keeps reverberating in my mind.

I have more reasons to be grateful. My injuries were minor considering the impact of the fall. Is it not a miracle that the huge aircraft met with substantial destruction whereas my fragile human body had injuries only in one leg which I could bear for so many hours? The infection and the fracture both could be treated, and recovery was possible well in time.

My upbringing had prepared me well for this because I was destined for this fate. My parents had pampered me but also made me tough. They had given me all the freedom to explore difficulties, get hurt, to endure pain and struggle. I do not remember a single incident where they had barred me from taking a risk or reprimanded me for getting injured. I had been taught by them to take responsibility for my actions and never regret the decisions once taken. And most importantly, they have taught us by leading, and never by preaching.

My Mom has always loved me unconditionally but never over-pampered me. As a child also, she would never fuss around me for little things. It might sound strange to many but till date she has not asked me any details of the accident. She will never put me through that experience ever again. This is real stoicism. And I respect her for this. Her focus after my return has only been on my recovery. I am very close to her and can communicate with her openly. Her biggest strength is that she is a patient listener. When she spoke to me for the first time after the surgery in the hospital room on video call, she only told me that she had full faith in me and that I would overcome every hurdle very soon.

My Dad would only prepare me for the next stage. He would anticipate all the imminent struggles and would suggest remedies. For instance, he had warned me about the frustration because of my immobility. He had suggested that I read books and practice meditation. He would even send links of motivational podcasts. We have come even closer after this episode. He has been my real-life hero since my childhood and now commands even more respect and love than ever before. I marvel at his attitude. He has stood by my side like a pillar of strength. He knows all that I have in my mind without me having to tell him. He fulfills my wishes even before I express them. He respects me as I am.

Fia, my sister, had held my hand and cried on the day I had returned from the US. She said that she had realized that she had never actually told me how much she loved me. She confessed that she had never said 'I love you, Brother!' ever before. Her tight hug conveyed all the unsaid love she has for me. She has not stopped fussing around me since the accident. Her sibling love has found manifestation in her gestures now. If you love someone, you must show your love as life is very unpredictable. Once gone, you will only live with the guilt and regret of not showing your love while you could. I have learnt to love my loved ones.

I have also learnt to let go of people. Sudden separation from all my friends who had stayed with me in the homestay are now in touch, but distance has cropped up between us. I had been in close touch with them when I returned to India and was confined to the bed. I used to talk to them all night. I made the first video call to *Diya* when I had started limping. I shared the pictures with *several others* when I wore my shoes again for the first time after the surgery. Even before going for the operation, I had texted them and received a prompt reply from them. Gradually the communication has diminished. They have become busy with their schedules, and I am busy with mine. Moreover, now the time zones are different. Although we talk less, we will remain good friends forever and the feelings are mutual.

Another discovery is that the world is a small place. If you are destined to achieve something or meet someone, no one can stop that. Two friends of mine, *Raghav* and *Mayur*, who I had met in *Bengaluru* while taking flying classes, were with me in *Florida* and now again, we were in the same class in *Delhi* where we prepared and appeared for the RTR examination. We had the same fun together as we used to have in the US. At the same time, we are far more professional than we were almost a year ago. We all have matured and are more focused on our goals in life.

My aim before going to the US was to become a skilful pilot but now it is to become a man of strong character as well. I now wish to live my life in a more productive manner. I want to be memorable to the people around me for good reasons. I want to be looked up to by my friends. I want to command respect from my fellow workers. The people who rescued me, who looked after me in the hospital and at the house in *Florida*—all are real super humans in my eyes. In their own eyes, they are ordinary people, who live ordinary lives and do good deeds not for recognition or appreciation but because they believe in doing noble deeds and that is their way of living life. I want to be like them.

I was a young teenager brimming with life ready to take over the world. The accident has changed it all. Now I am a wise young man ready to take over the world with more maturity, wisdom, and inner strength, who feels enlightened about his goals, with the realization that there is a long way to go in self-discovery. I shall broaden my vision and try to live a more fulfilling life even in the most ordinary fashion. I feel triumphant after the surgeries as I am overwhelmed with a sense of great pride and satisfaction. The pain and the suffering endured by me have made me view things with more clarity and value what I have in the present moment.

I am walking again, my friends are with me, flying classes in *Delhi* have resumed and I am very sure the enquiry will be in my favour, and I will fly back to *Florida*. Good times are ahead.

A quote by *Germany Kent* says it all for me.

"It's a funny thing about life, once you begin to take note of the things you are grateful for, you begin to lose sight of the things that you lack."

Looking forward to a life full of hope and faith.

A life which I wish to live with honesty and fortitude.

A life spent in doing even small deeds meaningfully and mindfully.

ARN TO FLY HERE!

"Survival is not just about enduring; it's about finding strength in the struggle, embracing the present moment, and being grateful for the breaths we take. Gratitude is the compass that guides us through life's darkest storms, reminding us that even in adversity, there's something to be thankful for."

– *Anonymous*

About the Author

Eshaan, a spirited 19-year-old, embarked on a daring journey from India to the sun-soaked swamps of *Florida*. His dream? To conquer the skies. Little did he know that fate had other plans—a brutal air crash in the unforgiving *Everglades*.

In the heart of danger, *Eshaan's* resilience shone. With a mangled Cessna, numbing cold, and lurking alligators, he fought for survival. His memoir captures not just the physical battle but the emotional turmoil—the primal instinct to live against all odds.

Eshaan's story transcends borders. It's a testament to courage, youth, and the indomitable human spirit. As you turn these pages, remember that survival isn't just about escaping death; it's about defying it.

Notes

1. After Eshaan returned to India after first three weeks of the crash, his heel was not getting healed. It had got infected, and the heel literally got separated from the foot. It is during this time he was operated upon by ***Dr. Nataraj H.M***, Sr. Consultant & Head Joint Replacement, Arthroscopy and Sports Specialist Surgeon at Belenus Champion hospital in Bengaluru.
2. ***Major D.P. Singh*** is a retired officer of the Indian Army. He is a Kargil War veteran and is known as India's first blade runner.
3. Bhagavad Gita 2.17
4. Bhagavad Gita 6.23
5. An old Yiddish saying, meaning "People plan, and God laughs."
6. Bhagavad Gita 2.47
7. *Assam* is a state in Northeastern India, south of the Eastern Himalayas along the Brahmaputra and Barak River valleys.
8. Agram Riding and Polo Academy is a Riding academy in Bengaluru in the Military area.

9. *Gurugram* is a satellite city and administrative headquarters of Gurgaon district, located in the northern Indian state of Haryana.
10. Zakhama is a small Naga village located approximately 18 km south of Kohima, the capital of Nagaland. Nagaland is a state in Northeast India.
11. Bengaluru is the capital and largest city of the southern Indian state of Karnataka.
12. Patiala is a city in Southeastern Punjab, Northwestern India. It is the fourth largest city in the state and is the administrative capital of Patiala district.
13. Chandigarh is a union territory and planned city in northern India, serving as the shared capital of the surrounding states, namely Punjab and Haryana. The master plan of the city was prepared by Swiss French architect Le Corbusier.
14. Remote Controlled
15. Bhagavad Gita 10.4
16. Vada pav is a popular and delicious Maharashtrian street food of fried batter coated potato dumplings sandwiched in a pav (soft dinner rolls).
17. A pilot check ride is the FAA practical test pilots must pass to receive a particular pilot certification or rating. The check ride is like a final exam after the pilot completes a course, such as the Private Pilot License (PPL) or Instrument Rating (IR).
18. Bhagavad Gita 3.35
19. Icarus, in Greek mythology, son of the inventor Daedalus who perished by flying too near the Sun with waxen wings.
20. Daedalus, mythical Greek inventor, architect, and sculptor who was said to have built the paradigmatic Labyrinth for King Minos of Crete.
21. Bhagavad Gita 16.1-3

22. Bhagavad Gita 2.27
23. Bhagavad Gita 2.69
24. Bhagavad Gita 3.18
25. Bhagavad Gita 2.48
26. Bhagavad Gita 16.3
27. Bhagavad Gita 8.62

www.ingramcontent.com/pod-product-compliance
Lightning Source LLC
LaVergne TN
LVHW091050150826
845673LV00002B/534

* 9 7 9 8 8 9 3 6 3 3 4 8 1 *